SUICIDE IN
RABBINIC LITERATURE

Suicide in Rabbinic Literature

by
Sidney Goldstein

KTAV PUBLISHING HOUSE, INC.
Hoboken, NJ

1/8/2008

Library of Congress Cataloging-in-Publication Data

Goldstein, Sidney, 1935–
     Suicide in Rabbinic literature / by Sidney Goldstein.
          p.   cm.
     Bibliography: p.
     Includes index.
     ISBN 0-88125-147-X
     1. Suicide — Religious aspects — Judaism.   2. Suicide in rabbinical
literature.   I. Title.
HV6545.G62 1988
296.3'85—dc19   88-13532
                                                                              CIP

Manufactured in the United States of America

Dedicated
to
Marilyn
Amy and Matt
Julie
Chaim Noach, Yaakov Koppel
and
Chava

Table of Contents

Introduction

Suicide is a major mental health problem in the United States. The *Journal of the American Medical Association* in a recent study indicates that nearly 25,000 deaths from suicide are recorded annually.[1] According to the National Institute of Mental Health, the actual figure is in all probability closer to 50,000.[2] If deaths occurring as a result of an overdose of drugs, alcoholism, and automobile accidents involving only a single person are added, the problem of suicide assumes even greater proportions.

My concern with the problem of suicide has evolved in the course of my professional responsibilities as chaplain at the Elmira Reformatory and the New York State Reception Center in Elmira, New York, and at the Marlboro State Hospital in Marlboro, New Jersey. At all three institutions I have counseled Jewish inmates and patients with suicidal tendencies.

In my capacity as rabbi, I have become aware of situations in which suicide victims have been denied certain burial and mourning rites. While this is unquestionably the Jewish law with regard to the culpable suicide, the present study will explore the parameters of that culpability.

The purpose of this study is to analyze and examine the attitudes and laws regarding suicide as indicated in the Judaic tradition. It traces these attitudes and laws from biblical times to the present and will cite and discuss the views of those who have dealt with the problem in their exegetical and halakhic works. The study will investigate the reasons and understandings underlying some of these views. It will examine precedents and discuss their applicability to contemporary situations. It will study the Judaic view of suicide committed as an act of martyrdom. I have briefly summarized the Greek, Roman, Christian, and psychiatric views of suicide in excursuses, so that comparisons with the Jewish view can be made when relevant.

With these objectives in mind, this study has utilized all the literature on the subject, including the Bible, biblical commentators, Apocrypha, Mishnah, Tosefta, M. *Semaḥot,* the Babylonian Talmud, Jerusalem Talmud, geonic and midrashic literature in addition to relevant talmudic commentators, codifiers, and responsa literature. Relevant historical works were also included when necessary. For the convenience of general readers, the most important texts, in translation, are assembled in the Appendix.

Bibliographical Essay

Studies of suicide in Jewish sources have heretofore been limited to brief analyses. In a booklet entitled *Eine Studie ueber den Selbstmord von juedischen Standpunkte*, A. Roth discusses the factors which can lead to suicide.[1] Part of the work is devoted to discussing the practice and attitudes of Judaism in helping to prevent suicide. There is no extensive analysis of the laws of mourning with regard to a suicide found in rabbinic literature, nor is there any analysis of why certain suicides are inculpable. Roth indicates, in this work, that suicide is obligatory when one is required to commit idolatry, adultery, or murder. I shall demonstrate in this study that the sources dealing with this matter do not mandate that one kill oneself to avoid transgressing these precepts.

In an article entitled "Der Selbstmord nach der Halacha," A. Perls discusses the meaning of the term *b'da'at* and cites examples in midrashic and talmudic literature where this word is found. Perls indicates that in these sources as well as in those that deal with suicide, *b'da'at* ("with knowledge") has the connotation of a willful act or response.[2]

Perhaps in response to the recent rise in reported suicides among Jews, there has been an increase in articles on the subject of late. Under the heading of "Suicide," the *Encyclopaedia Judaica* contains two articles. The first, by L. I. Rabinowitz, cites the suicides in the Bible, Josephus (Masada), and York. The definition of intentional suicide is stipulated, and some contemporary applications of the laws of inculpable suicides are stated.[3]

Rabinowitz states that suicide "is nowhere explicitly forbidden in the Talmud." This, however, is not the case, as indicated in *Baba Kamma* 91b. A further statement indicates that "four definite suicides are recorded in the Bible. Samson, Saul and his armor-bearer, and Ahithophel." As I demonstrate in this work, Samson is not treated as a suicide in the rabbinic literature dealing with his death. With regard to Masada, Rabinowitz claims: "It has been suggested that they acted in accordance with their interpretation of the *halakhah* which included slavery and subjection to a foreign power as one of those principles concerning which one was enjoined 'to be killed rather than transgress.' " This is a farfetched assumption. With very few exceptions there is no association of the martyrdom mentioned in the Talmudic passage of *yehareg v'al ya'avor* ("letting oneself be killed rather than sin") with suicide. Slavery and subjection to a foreign power would certainly not obligate one to commit suicide. There are other parallels to Masada, wherein individuals took their lives rather than allow themselves to be subjected to acts of immorality.[4] If slavery involved subjection to immoral practices, these might serve as valid precedents. The sugya of *yehareg v'al ya'avor* ("letting oneself be killed rather than sin"), however, does not entirely explain the suicides at Masada.

In a second article, Haim Cohn discusses the factor of duress in the adjudication of a suicide.[5] His delineation of the factors of duress is well done, although incomplete. His statement that "the law was settled to the effect that where [one] is required to commit idolatry, adultery . . . or murder, he must kill himself or let himself be killed rather than commit any of those crimes" is not supported by the sources dealing with this matter.

In an important Hebrew article, "Hitavdut mida'at b'mikra u'bisafrut ha-rabbanit" ("Suicide in the Bible and Rabbinical Literature"), C. Reines discusses the social and psychological elements of suicide as well as some of the philosophical discussions relating to it. He stresses the subjective elements relating to suicide and cites sources in rabbinic literature which discuss suicide as an act of repentance, and analyzes them well.[6] He does not discuss the problems posed by the mass suicides at Masada, nor does he deal with suicide as an act of martyrdom.

Reines's English article, "The Jewish View of Suicide," contains much of the same material as the Hebrew article.[7] This article, however, is less comprehensive than the one written in Hebrew.

Fred Rosner, in a chapter "Suicide in Biblical, Talmudic, and Rabbinic Writings," reviews instances of suicide in the Bible, Apocrypha, and talmudic literature. Some relevant codes are mentioned.[8] There is little analysis of any of the sources cited.

In a chapter entitled "Suicide in Jewish Perspective," David Novak discusses the source of the prohibition of suicide and differentiates between suicide and martyrdom.[9] There is no citation and discussion of sources on suicide as an act of martyrdom in the medieval period. Novak points to mental illness as an exculpatory factor in suicide and correctly notes the early association of mental imbalance with suicide in Judaic sources. He indicates that King Saul is the paradigm of the "psychotic suicide." The sources, however, indicate that Saul's suicide was not brought about by any psychotic distortions of reality (i.e., hallucinations, paranoia, or the like) but rather by the very tragic and uncompromising circumstances in which he found himself. This is further demonstrated by the fact that many authorities utilized Saul as the prototype for suicide under stressful conditions which were definitely within the realm of reality—debts, incarceration, poverty, and so on.

Maurice Lamm, in *The Jewish Way of Death and Mourning*, discusses procedures for determining the culpability of a suicide and cites factors which would render a suicide inculpable. Mourning rites for the suicide are delineated.[10] In *Yesodai Smochot*, Aaron Felder discusses the laws of mourning for a suicide victim.[11] Rabbi Y. Greenwald has written two texts, each of which contains a brief treatment of the Jewish view of suicide. He reviews the opinions of various authorities. In addition, he cites circumstances of suicide and the determination of these cases.[12]

In his compendium on the laws of mourning, Rabbi J. Tuktzinski devotes part of a chapter to the laws of suicide. His discussion is far more thorough than that of his colleagues.[13]

Rabbi Jacob Ginsberg, in his work *Mishpatim L'yisrael*, discusses certain interesting elements related to suicide. With reference to mercy killing, Rabbi Ginsberg states that one who kills an infirm person, even at the person's request, is still to be considered a murderer. With regard to punishment for a person saved from a suicide attempt, R. Ginsberg determined that the decision should be left to the court's discretion. The text states that no individual is allowed to place himself in conditions wherein his life or health would be endangered. It also indicates that an individual has the responsibility of saving a suicide attempter's life. In the event of a duel, Rabbi Ginsberg determined that the individual who kills another is guilty of murder. This is his view even if there was a mutual understanding, which preceded the duel, that the "winner" would not be punished.

Rabbi Ginsberg bases his decisions on the view that the individual is not the sole master of his body; he therefore can neither do as he pleases with himself nor tell others to harm him.[14]

Suicides as acts of martyrdom have been recorded and documented in various historical works which deal with Jewish life in Christian Europe.[15]

There are also contemporary works which cite incidents of suicide as acts of martyrdom.[16] I shall seek to place these accounts within the framework of the Jewish view of suicide, as indicated in biblical, talmudic, and rabbinic sources.

In this work I have attempted to present a comprehensive study of the subject of suicide as found in Jewish sources. Despite the many valuable articles and sections of books written on this subject, a comprehensive study is at present lacking.

Acknowledgments

The author has many to thank for their magnanimous help and support in reaching this achievement in his life.

My grandparents, Mr. and Mrs. Yitzhak Zbarsky of blessed memory, were a very important influence in my life. My grandfather was a dedicated Hebraist, devoted to the study of Hebrew language and literature. I shall always be in their debt for their commitment and concern for my welfare.

I should like to thank my parents, Mr. and Mrs. Herman Goldstein for always providing me with a Jewish education. This work is but a small result of their manifold efforts and sacrifices in my behalf. I deeply regret that my father did not live to see this publication. I know, however, that he would have fully shared in the exhilaration of its completion.

My deep appreciation is extended to my dear in-laws, Mr. and Mrs. Ephraim Wurtzel for their warm and sympathetic support all during the travail and tribulations associated with my years of research.

The same is true of my sister and brother-in-law, Drs. and Mrs. Paul Diament, and my sister-in-law and brother-in-law, Dr. and Mrs. H. Daniel Roth.

A special thanks to my sister, Dr. Carol Diament for her perusal of the manuscript and the many beneficial insights she offered.

My sincere thanks are extended to Dr. Meyer Feldblum, University Professor of Talmudic Literature at Yeshiva University for sharing his vast erudition with me. His great knowledge and understanding were often critical in the development of this study.

To the members of the Psychiatry Department at Albert Einstein Medical Center, Northern Division and Philadelphia

Psychiatric Center, Dr. Paul Fink, Chairman; Dr. Harold Bitman, Dr. Leonardo Magran, Dr. Joshua Werblowsky, my gratitude is extended for their many helpful ideas and suggestions.

I am also most grateful to friends and colleagues, Dr. Louis H. Feldman, Professor of Classics at Yeshiva University, Dr. Samuel Lachs, Professor of Judaic Studies at Bryn Mawr College, Rabbi Norman Singer of Congregation Oheb Sholom, Williamsport, PA., and Instructor of Judaic Studies at Lycoming College and Dr. Nahum Waldman, Professor of Biblical Literature at Gratz College, Philadelphia, PA., for their many helpful and insightful ideas.

A deep debt of gratitude which cannot be truly articulated I owe to my beloved children, Amy and Julie. They gave far more of themselves in support, encouragement and cooperation than any father has a right to expect. For all the times which this project kept me from involvement with them, I am truly sorry, for their unstinting love, warmth and daughterly affection, I am profoundly indebted.

I simply could not and would not have completed this study without the constant support of my beloved wife, Marilyn. She truly was partner, critic, editor, analyst and friend throughout this difficult journey.

Needless to say any errors are solely attributable to myself and in no way reflect the suggestions of any of those kind enough to be of help.

The Memorial Foundation for Jewish Culture contributed graciously towards the research of this work, as did the Achkenazi Brothers Foundation of Deal, N.J. I am most appreciative of their kind assistance, as well as that of the sponsorship of my mother.

Finally my humble thanks are offered to the Almighty for providing me with the strength, health and determination to complete this task. May he continue to give me the strength to further contribute to the understanding, teaching and elucidation of His Torah.

Philadelphia
Sivan 5748
June 1988

SUICIDE IN
RABBINIC LITERATURE

Chapter 1

Suicide in Biblical and Exegetical Literature

The Bible does not have an explicit prohibition against suicide. The following verse has been interpreted in the Talmud as the prohibition of suicide:[1]

> And surely your blood of your lives will I require; at the hand of every beast will I require it; and at the hand of man, even at the hand of every man's brother, will I require the life of man.[2]

In Baba Kamma, R. Eleazar is quoted as saying: "I will require your blood if taken by your own hands."[3] The Midrash mentions prominent exceptions to this prohibition.[4] It cites the situations of King Saul and of Hananiah, Mishael, and Azariah.[5] The Targumim do not mention either the midrashic or the talmudic understanding in their translation of Genesis 9:5. They interpret the verse in a literal sense, i.e., "The blood which is your lives will I require."[6] Various other translations as well do not interpret Genesis 9:5 as indicating a prohibition against suicide.[7]

One of the problems which faced the biblical commentators with regard to this verse is its congruity with the text in which it is found. The preceding verses, Genesis 9:1–4, deal with the Almighty's declaration to Noah and his sons, giving them dominion over all living things and prohibiting them from partaking of blood. The verses which follow Genesis 9:5 speak of the punishment of the murderer through the agency of

other men (i.e., the courts or an avenger). The section concludes with a blessing to Noah and his sons to "be fruitful and
multiply." What does Genesis 9:5 indicate within this context?

The biblical commentators who have dealt with this passage
can be divided into three groups.

In the first group, Rashi explains the text, utilizing the
talmudic and midrashic interpretation. In his view the first part
of Genesis 9:5 prohibits suicide even in the absence of blood.[8]

R. Solomon b. Abraham Parḥon adds an important theological view to the talmudic and midrashic explanation. Man's soul
and body do not belong to him alone, and consequently he
cannot do with them as he pleases. The gravity of the sin of
killing oneself is therefore equal to that of killing another, as in
both situations one is taking that which is not his. Parḥon
admonishes against jeopardizing one's own well-being through
placing oneself in dangerous circumstances, e.g., in the vicinity
of wild beasts, as this might result in one's losing one's life. In
his view, an animal is exonerated if it injures or kills a man, as it
has not been warned against doing so, but in the world-to-
come, the Almighty will demand the blood of the one who
endangered himself by exposure to wild beasts and other
hazards.[9]

R. Joseph Bekhor Shor interprets the first clause of Genesis
9:5 as prohibiting suicide. In his view, the phrase *miyad kol haya
edreshenu* ("at the hand of every beast will I require it") specifically indicates the animal's culpability when it kills or injures
man.[10]

A number of commentators who fall into this category
stressed various words in the verse to bolster their interpretation. R. Baḥya understood the word *l'nafshoteykham* ("of your
souls") as *minafshoteykhem*, i.e., "from your souls." The Almighty
in this view says: "If you take your life, I will demand it from
your souls."[11]

R. Meir Loeb Malbim explains the word *ḥaya*, usually interpreted as "beast," as referring to the eternal soul, from which
the Almighty will demand punishment.[12]

Certain commentators were concerned with the issue of

punishment for the suicide. Through his action, the suicide placed himself beyond the justice of any earthly court. Yet how could he be allowed to go unpunished for such a heinous deed? R. Hezekiah b. Manoah therefore understands Genesis 9:5 as proof that there is in fact a world-to-come.[13]

R. Jacob Z. Mecklenburg explains the severity of the crime of suicide, and its consequent punishment, in a twofold manner:

> 1. A person who committed suicide in a willful fashion will not be forgiven even if he possessed Torah learning and good deeds.

> 2. The punishment for suicide is more severe than that for *karet* (excision). With reference to *karet* there is no loss of the soul itself. With reference to suicide the soul itself will be utterly destroyed.[14]

It is possible that Mecklenburg was responding to contemporaneous situations wherein individuals who were learned and charitable had indeed taken their lives. There does not seem to be any other reason for his stressing this point. Similarly, this might be his motivation in describing the severity of the punishment of the suicide. He, after all, brings no evidence as to why he considers suicide even more severe than *karet*. Perhaps this is an attempt on his part to admonish any potential suicides and present them with the terrible consequences of their deed.[15]

A second group of commentators first give their own understanding of the verse and then cite the rabbinic interpretation.

Nahmanides understands Genesis 9:5 as intimating that one incurs the death penalty for spilling the blood upon which life depends but not for spilling the blood of those limbs on which life is not dependent. Nahmanides adds: "Our Rabbis have expounded this verse as an injunction against suicide."[16]

R. David Kimhi explains the first phrases of Genesis 9:5 as referring to the punishment of animals who take human life.

He then cites the rabbinic interpretation as well. [17] The rabbinic interpretation of this verse appended to the understandings of these commentators would seem to indicate their difficulty in accepting only the rabbinic explanation.

The third group either does not make any mention of the rabbinic interpretation or denies its validity. R. Abraham Ibn Ezra rejects the rabbinic interpretation. He feels that the interpretation of this verse which indicates suicide is farfetched.[18]

S. D. Luzzatto disputes the rabbinic explanation of this verse as prohibiting suicide. In his view, since the text does not read *minafshoteykhem* ("from your souls") but rather *l'nafshshoteykhim* ("of your souls"), there is no basis for the prohibition of suicide. In addition, he says, the rabbinic explanation has no connection with the next clause, *miyad kol ḥaya edreshenu* ("from every animal will I demand it").[19]

Abrabanel, Sforno, R. Moses Alsheik, and R. Naftali Zvi Yehudah Berlin (among others) do not mention suicide at all with reference to Genesis 9:5.[20]

There are wide discrepancies in the exegetical literature dealing with Genesis 9:5. The primary difference lies in whether the talmudic and midrashic interpretation is considered to be the meaning of the verse. If it is, then various questions follow. What is the status of a suicide in which no blood is shed? Can there be any punishment for a suicide? Are there other words in Genesis 9:5, besides the first five, which might also point to its reference to suicide?

If the talmudic and midrashic interpretaion is not accepted as the meaning of Genesis 9:5, then the verse primarily serves as an admonition against the taking of human life.[21]

While it is true that some biblical commentators did not accept the talmudic and midrashic explanation, research has shown that the halakhic authorities utilized these talmudic and midrashic interpretations to render their decisions with regard to cases of suicide. This will be demonstrated throughout this study, and the implications and ramifications will be discussed at length.

Chapter 2

Instances of Suicide in the Prophets, Writings, and Apocrypha

Incidents indicative of suicide are cited in the Prophets. Scholars have considered Samson to be such an example.[1] In a last act of defiance Samson asked to be taken to the pillars on which the Philistine place of assembly rested.

> And Samson called unto the Lord, and said: "O Lord God, remember me, I pray Thee, and strengthen me, I pray Thee, only this once, O God, that I may be this once avenged of the Philistines for my two eyes. . . . And Samson said: "Let me die with the Philistines." And he bent with all his might; and the house fell upon the lords, and upon all the people that were therein. So the dead that he slew at his death were more than they that he slew in his life.[2]

The Talmud and Midrash viewed the events as divine intervention on Samson's behalf, due either to the righteousness of his forefathers and/or to the unselfish quality of his leadership of Israel; they make no comment as to the suicidal aspects of his actions, nor do they evaluate his behavior on this basis.

Samson is viewed in the Midrash as possessing a source of strength originally granted to him by Isaac in his blessing to Jacob.[3] The Talmud attributes Samson's final surge of strength to the unselfish and egalitarian quality of his leadership of Israel.[4] Samson's final statement is viewed by the Targum as a prayer which was answered, culminating in his self-destructive act.[5] Kimḥi clearly sees Samson's death as redeeming his entire

7

career as a Judge of Israel.[6] R. Levi b. Gershon also understands Samson's death as a final triumphant deed which placed an affirmative stamp on his leadership of Israel.[7]

Samson's death evoked a positive reaction in the Talmud, Midrash, and certain biblical commentators. There is no condemnation of his death as a suicide even though it was obviously self-inflicted. On the contrary, it is viewed as a redemptive deed. In addition, it is seen as an answer to the religious act of prayer. Most halakhic authorities do not utilize his case in their discussions of the topic of suicide, as is the case with King Saul.[8] The conclusion can be drawn that in rabbinic literature, Samson's last act is not viewed as a suicide but as an act of great martial courage, and the fact that is was actually a self-inflicted death was not of primary significance.[9]

A paradigm of suicide is the case of King Saul. The final battle of Saul's life was against the Philistines on Mount Gilboa. His three sons had been killed. His military position had become untenable, as he was surrounded by Philistine archers.[10] Fearing abuse and debasement if he were to be captured alive, he asked his armor-bearer to kill him.[11] The armor-bearer refused. "Therefore Saul took his sword, and fell upon it. And when his armor-bearer saw that Saul was dead, he likewise fell upon his sword, and died with him."[12] A somewhat contradictory account is later related by an Amalekite youth to David. The youth told David that he had killed Saul.[13]

The Book of Chronicles relates the events in accordance with the first account (1 Samuel 31:1–7). There is no mention of the Amalekite's involvement.[14]

The Midrash understood Saul's death to be the result of his heeding Samuel's instruction. It stresses his obedience to authority. Samuel told Saul that if he fell by the sword, his death would be an act of atonement and he would dwell with Samuel in "his compartment," i.e., in Paradise.[15]

Another midrashic source described the Almighty as approving Saul's acceptance of Samuel's admonition.[16] The rabbinic sources are not concerned with the suicidal aspects of the final moments of Saul's life. The texts deal with his death as an act of atonement which came about through his acceding to

Samuel's authority. They also praise his gracious acceptance of the terrible decree. Samuel's prophecy was fulfilled with gruesome effectiveness. The texts do not focus on Saul's suicide because of the view that death was projected to him as a viable option, bringing reward in its wake, and was in actuality preordained. His suicide was the consummation of all these elements and did not in and of itself require justification or discussion.

The commentators, however, discuss the matter of Saul's death at length. They demonstrate much perplexity about the events surrounding it and question its permissibility.

Mevasser b. Nissi HaBavli cites Saadia Gaon, who questioned Saul's death. How could Saul have killed himself? Was he not considered God's chosen one? (How could he have done what was prohibited?) Saadia responds to this question by indicating that the Amalekite killed him. Saadia obviously could not accept Saul's death as occurring through a suicide.[17] The Midrash makes a specific exception in Saul's case.[18] Nevertheless, Saadia preferred to understand Saul's death as perpetrated by the Amalekite, in order to remove any question with regard to the appropriateness of Saul's demise.

R. David Kimhi at first selects the option of the Amalekite taking Saul's life. He also accepts the possibility that Saul may have killed himself and that the Amalekite lied to find favor in David's eyes.[19]

The question remains, however, how could Saul take his own life? Is it not expressly prohibited in Genesis 9:5?

Kimhi responds to this in a twofold manner. He points to the inevitability of Saul's death, since Samuel had prophesied that he would die. Kimhi also indicates that the stress that Saul experienced had reached such a point that he preferred death at his own hand rather than to be violated by the Philistines.[20]

According to Kimhi's first explanation of why Saul killed himself, Saul's case is exceptional and unique and probably could not serve as a model for understanding other cases of suicide. According to his second explanation, Saul's case might serve as a prototype of suicide because he took his life due to great duress. This understanding has often served later authorities as a basis for decisions rendered in cases of suicide.

Abrabanel is also perplexed by Saul's suicide and by the question of who actually killed him.[21] He, at first, combines the inevitability of Saul's death with the psychological distress that he understood Saul to have suffered. In his view, Saul was afraid that he would be wounded and rendered incapable of defending himself. Saul envisioned that the Philistines would cut off parts of his body because of the intense hatred they had for him. He preferred, then, to die at the hand of an ally rather than be killed by his enemies. Since his armor-bearer did not want to kill him, he took his own life.

Abrabanel, though, in a second interpretation, indicates that Saul did not die immediately from his self-inflicted wound. The Amalekite youth actually killed him. He feels that this is the more accurate version.

Abrabanel specifically frees Saul from any onus of sin because of his suicide, as his death was preordained and escape was impossible. He does, however, add another dimension. Saul esteemed honor and status. Since he knew that he would be terribly abused, death contained less terror for him than his envisoned torture.[22]

Abrabanel adds another understanding to the stress that Saul encountered: the subjective psychological stress of one in high position who sees his status deteriorating and about to be lost.

This has important implications which will be discussed in later sections of this study.

Another case of suicide, in the Prophets, involves Ahithophel, the counselor of King David, who turned against the king and sided with his rebellious son, Absalom. The following account is given:

> And when Ahithophel saw that his counsel was not followed, he saddled his ass, and arose, and got him home, unto his city, and set his house in order, and strangled himself, and he died, and was buried in the sepulchre of his father.[23]

The Talmud sees an element of preordination in Ahithophel's death. The statement "the curse of a sage though uttered without cause takes effect" is applied to Ahithophel.[24] David sought an answer to a particular question. When no one responded, he said: "Whoever knows anything on this topic and does not tell, will be suffocated." Ahithophel did supply the appropriate answer. Yet the Talmud concludes: "Nevertheless it is recorded that Ahithophel . . . hanged himself and died."[25]

Some of the commentators see Ahithophel's suicide as politically and economically motivated.

R. David Kimḥi suggests that he chose to kill himself rather than to be killed by David. This, he felt, was his only alternative, since his advice had not been accepted, and Absalom and his forces would fall into David's hands.[26] R. Meir Loeb Malbim explains that Ahithophel was afraid that David would kill him because he would consider him an instigator of rebellion, and then his properties would accrue to the king, as was the law with one executed by the king. Therefore, he strangled himself to save his properties for his heirs.[27] These commentators, then, do not see an exclusivity related to Ahithophel's case. They understand it as the reaction of a desperate man to an untenable situation.

The Mishnah in *Sanhedrin* indicates that "Ahithophel has no share in the world-to-come."[28] The Talmud does not indicate why Ahithophel was excluded from a share in the world-to-come. It may be because he had committed treason and not because he had taken his own life.

Another possible instance of suicide in the Bible is that of Zimri.

> And it came to pass, when Zimri saw that the city was taken, that he went into the castle of the king's house and burnt the king's house over him with fire and he died.[29]

The text, however, is ambiguous. Omri, who was Zimri's rival, had laid siege to his position and had trapped him. The passage can be understood in two ways—either that Zimri burned the house over himself or that Omri did. R. David Kimḥi is of the opinion that Omri perpetrated this act.[30]

The Second Book of Maccabees mentions an act of suicide by a Jew. It is cited with approval and praise.

The representative of King Demetrius, Nicanor, in order to demoralize the Jewish population of Jerusalem, ordered that one of Jerusalem's most honored residents, Razis, be seized. Razis, rather than capitulate, "fell upon his own sword, preferring to die nobly, rather than to fall into the hands of sinners, and suffer outrages unworthy of his noble birth."[31]

This may reflect the influence of some comtemporaneous elements in Greek culture which viewed suicide favorably.[32]

The material presented in this chapter suggests that Samson's death should be considered as occurring due to an act of war rather than as an act of suicide.

Saul's case, however, presents some interesting problems. In rabbinic literature his death is considered an act of atonement. Is suicide as an act of atonement acceptable? Rabbinic literature, and to an even greater extent the biblical commentators, point to the inevitability of Saul's death. This is one of the reasons that Saul is not considered an intentional suicide.[33] This raises some important questions. Does the principle of inevitability apply to a supernatural element (e.g., Samuel's prophecy or David's curse), in which case Saul's death would present a unique situation which could not serve as a model for any other case of suicide?

Can it also be applied to one whose physical condition is such that he is given no chance to live? Is such an inevitability considered a sufficient reason for one to take his own life? If one took his own life in these circumstances, is he considered an intentional and consequently culpable suicide?

Saul is also understood to have been under tremendous stress. If the stress factor is considered valid, how widely can it be applied and to what circumstances? How far can the principle of subjectivity be taken with regard to a suicide? The approaches of the rabbinic literature and biblical commentators to the suicides in the Prophets can serve as a basis for a contemporary understanding of the Jewish attitude toward suicide. This will be demonstrated in the course of this study.

Chapter 3

Suicide in Talmudic Literature

In general tannaitic literature, the subject of suicide, and the rites associated with it, is not discussed. However, tannaitic sources in *Semaḥot* discuss the ritual procedures for a suicide.[1]

The text of *Semaḥot* states unequivocally, "For a suicide no rites whatsoever should be observed."[2] To emphasize the sense of distaste with which such an act is viewed, the text states that R. Ishmael said: "He may be lamented: 'Alas, misguided fool! Alas, misguided fool!' "[3]

R. Akiba (perhaps to spare the unfortunate family more suffering) said: "Leave him to his oblivion, neither bless him nor curse him."[4]

The rites which are not to be observed are enumerated. "There may be no rending of clothes, no baring of shoulders, no eulogizing for him."[5]

However, the feelings of the bereaved survivors are taken into account. "But people should line up for him and the mourner's blessing should be recited over him, out of respect for the living."[6]

To underline the concern for the survivors, and to establish a viable principle, the baraita concludes: "The general rule is: the public should participate in whatsoever is done out of respect for the living. It should not participate in whatsoever is done out of respect for the dead."[7] Obviously, then, a death occurring as a result of a suicide is to be treated in a special way, in a manner different from the way in which the deceased was usually dealt with in Judaic tradition.

Who is to be considered an intentional suicide? This study will show that throughout the rabbinic literature dealing with this subject, there are many qualifications, questions of intent, extenuating and mitigating circumstances, and the like, which often precluded labeling a decedent as a culpable suicide. *Semaḥot* explores the possibilities and determines that a culpable suicide, subject to halakhic penalties, is one carried out through responsible choice, with intent definitely stated by the perpetrator and clearly understood by the listener. Anything else is not within the realm of a culpable suicide. The crucial halakhic question, then, is: Was the act done *b'da'at* or *shelo b'da'at*? Was it done with deliberate intent or not?

The text of *Semaḥot* makes this point very clearly. It says, "Who is to be accounted a suicide?"

> Not one who climbs to the top of a tree or to the top of a roof, and falls to his death.[8] Rather, it is one who says, "Behold, I am going to climb to the top of the tree, or to the top of the roof, and then throw myself down to my death," and thereupon others see him climb to the top of the tree, or to the top of the roof, and fall to his death."[9]

After premeditation has been clearly and definitely established in this fashion, then "such a one is presumed to be a suicide, and for such a person no rites whatsoever should be observed."[10]

To further stress the absolute need for clear intent, we are told in the passage immediately following: "If a person is found strangled from a tree, or slain impaled upon a sword, he is presumed to have taken his life unwittingly. To such a person no rites whatsoever may be denied."[11]

That is to say, even though circumstances and available evidence may lead one to feel that the individual took his own life deliberately, there is no operative presumption (*hazakah*) which would compel us to determine that the act was a deliberate one and consequently culpable.

The text of *Semaḥot* then provides two illustrations which demonstrate the absence of culpability with regard to a suicidal act:

It happened that the son of Gorgos[12]ran away from school. His father threatened to box his ears. In terror of his father, the boy went off and cast himself into a cistern. The incident was brought before R. Tarfon, who ruled "no rites whatsoever are to be denied him."[13]

A similar case is also cited, that of a child from Bene Berak who broke a flask. His father threatened to box his ears. In terror of his father, the child went off and cast himself into a cistern. The matter was brought before Rabbi Akiba, who ruled: "No rites whatsoever are to be denied him." As a result of this, the Sages said: "A man should not threaten his child. He should spank him at once, or hold his peace, and say nothing."[14]

The reason for the lack of culpability in these cases is a subject of debate by later authorities. Naḥmanides interprets the case of the son of Gorgos as representing the suicide of a minor. He is not culpable because a child is not considered to have the capacity of responsible judgment in order to act deliberately. R. Tarfon, in Naḥmanides' view, ruled that "no rites whatsoever are to be denied him" because he was a minor, which is equivalent to an adult acting in an irrational manner.[15]

Asheri indicates that the question here is not the inculpability of a minor. Jewish law generally renders a minor inculpable.[16] Viewing the son of Gorgos as a minor does not support the previous baraita, which dealt with the unwitting and, consequently, inculpable suicide of an adult. The baraitas are linked, as the text reads: *uma'aseh bivno shel Gorgiyos* ("And it happened that the son of Gorgos").[17] The son of Gorgos should therefore be understood as an unwitting adult suicide similar to one found fallen on his sword. His inculpability stems from the fact that he was driven by fear and panic to take his life.[18]

Utilizing Asheri's reasoning, the suicide involving the child from Bene Berak can be understood as not referring to a minor. The word *tinok* ("child") used in this situation also refers to one who has reached the age of majority.[19] Even though the individual was no longer a minor, he was deemed inculpable because of the intense fear of his father that impelled him to take his life.

Naḥmanides understands the baraitas of the son of Gorgos and the child of Bene Berak to be sufficiently supportive of the one dealing with the unwitting adult suicide because in his view they are the same. There is no difference between the unwitting adult suicide and the suicides of the minors. In both cases, culpable intention was lacking. Asheri views the baraitas of the son of Gorgos and the child of Bene Berak as possibly contradicting the baraita of the unwitting adult suicide, because they are dealing with two separate and distinct legal situations. Consequently, in his view, both baraitas (the one dealing with the son of Gorgos and that dealing with the child of Bene Berak) discuss adults. In that way they are analogous with the previous one because intent was lacking. The lack of intent was due to panic and fear rather than to their not having reached the age of majority. This early association of suicide with irrational behavior is most significant and has greatly influenced the views of many authorities in dealing with cases of suicide.

Chapter 4

The Definition of Intentional Suicide by Talmudic Commentators and Codifiers

The definition of intentional suicide as delineated in *Semaḥot* is as follows:

> Who is to be accounted a suicide? Not one who climbs to the top of a tree or to the top of a roof, and falls to his death. Rather it is one who says, "Behold, I am going to climb to the top of the tree, or to the top of the roof, and then throw myself down to my death," and thereupon, others see him climb to the top of the tree, or to the top of the roof and fall to his death. Such a one is presumed to be a suicide, and for such a person no rites whatsoever should be observed.[1]

There are several critical phrases in the preceding passage.

1. Rather it is one who says, "Behold, I am going to climb to the top of the tree or to the edge of the roof, and *then throw myself down to my death.*"[2]

2. . . . and thereupon, *others see him* climb to the top of the tree . . . and fall to his death.

3. Such a one is *presumed to be a suicide.*

The text requires a full statement of intention, followed by an action, which was witnessed by others. Given this, there is then the presumption (*hazakah*) that the individual took his life with deliberate intention (*b'da'at*).[3]

Two of the extant versions of the *Baal Halakhot G'dolot* (Bahag) have the following text, which is different from that of *Semaḥot:*

> Rather, one who says, "See that I am going to climb to the roof in order (*al m'nat*) to fall."[4]

The term *alm'nat* is associated with a condition (*t'nai*.) A condition bases a transaction or a relationship on very specific stipulations.[5] These versions of the Bahag may be indicating that the statement of an intentional suicide must be tied solely to the condition that he is ascending to the roof to fall from it. Since the above versions of the Bahag require this sort of statement, there may not be a need for witnesses to his fall. His very specific statement is sufficient reason to establish the presumption that he took his life with deliberate intention.

Alfasi's text of the statement of the intentional suicide contains neither the phrase *v'apil azmi v'amut* ("and I will throw myself down to my death") nor the phrase *al m'nat lipoel* ("in order to fall"). He writes: "Rather, he says, 'Behold, I am going to climb up to the roof,' and they saw him climb to the top of the roof, and he fell and died. Such a one is presumed to be a suicide."[6] He requires that the individual be seen ascending to the roof. The presumption is operative when a statement of intent is enunciated and the ascension is witnessed.

Maimonides requires a declaration similar to Alfasi's of the intentional suicide. "Behold, I am going to climb to the top of the roof." Maimonides then writes: "They saw that he immediately climbed up in an angry manner or fearfully, fell and died; such a one is presumed to be a suicide."[7] He is pointing here to the principle of immediacy (*miyad*). Maimonides also cites the principle of immediacy with regard to the validity of a divorce. A man in good health said, "Write a *get* for my wife." The *get* was written, sealed, and given to her, after which he immediately killed himself. The *get* was considered valid despite the fact that he did not specify that it be given to his wife.[8]

A commentator has understood this to be similar to the case

of one who was very ill and asked that a *get* be written for his wife without specifying that it be given to her. In the latter case, the *get* was considered valid because the individual was thought to be too debilitated to indicate that the *get* be given to his wife. In the former case, his immediate suicide indicates that the individual was too confused to specify that the *get* be given to his wife.[9]

Immediacy, then, is considered valid proof of a person's intention. Maimonides applies this understanding specifically to a case of suicide. The individual's ascent to the roof immediately after he indicated that he would do so, and his subsequent fall, are proof of his intention to take his life. It has been suggested by a nineteenth-century Ashkenazic authority that Maimonides requires immediacy to establish the intentional suicide because the statement he requires in the case of a suicide is a limited one: *r'u she'ani oleh l'rosh hagag* ("Look, I am climbing to the top of the roof"). He does not require that the purpose of the ascent be stipulated. Consequently, immediacy is necessary to verify the intent.[10]

In addition to the element of immediacy, Maimonides specifies consideration of the individual's mood at the time of his ascent to the roof. Demonstration of anger or fear is considered further proof of suicidal intent.

The stipulations "in an angry way" (*derekh ka'as*) and "he was afraid" (*shehaya meizar*) indicate that these are *not* exonerating factors. On the contrary, they contribute to an individual's culpability as an intentional suicide.[11]

Nahmanides does not require that the person be seen ascending the roof or falling from it. In his view, a statement of intent is sufficient to label him an intentional suicide.

Nahmanides' text reads: "But [a suicide] is one who says, 'See, I am climbing the tree,' and he falls and dies, 'to the top of the roof,' and he falls and dies; he is presumed to be a suicide[12] even if others did not see him jump; since he made this utterance, he creates the presumption that [this] was intentional."

Asheri has added another dimension to the statement of

intent. He requires that the person specifically state his intention to die. "[Rather] one who says, 'Behold, I am going to climb to the top of the roof, and *I will jump to my death*,' and they saw that he did climb to the top of the roof, and fell and died. In this case there is a presumption that he committed suicide."[13]

An additional observation is in order with regard to the text of *Semaḥot*. The text stipulates an individual *"climbing to the top of the tree, or to the top of the roof."* This suggests that *Semaḥot* originally postulated a *clear demonstration* so that there would be further evidence of an individual's intent.

The primary question with regard to the intentional suicide is whether a viable presumption of intention exists. I suggest that this is the basic difference in the texts of the commentators. *Each has a different requirement in order to establish the presumption.* The versions of the Bahag cited seek a most specific kind of statement. Alfasi requires a less specific statement but stipulates that witnesses must see him fall to his death after his pronouncement. Maimonides mentions a few conditions which his predecessors did not cite. Immediacy and the person's mood at the time of his ascent to the roof are the factors he adds to the determination of the intentional suicide. Naḥmanides requires *only* a statement of intent to establish the presumption as viable. Asheri requires a clear statement, with the reason for the ascent explicitly indicated. This must be witnessed by others. It is then that the individual is considered an intentional suicide.

The commentators established specific criteria for judging an act of suicide as intentional. In order to override the basic presumption of innocence which exists with regard to every individual,[14] the suicide would have to conform with those criteria.

According to *Semaḥot*, where there is no evidence that helps to establish a presumption of intentional suicide, an individual who has taken his own life is considered to have done so unwittingly, due to the basic presumption of innocence which applies to him. "If a person is found strangled and hanging from a tree, or slain impaled upon a sword, he is presumed to have taken his life unwittingly, and [as to] anyone who takes his life unwittingly, no [burial or mourning rites] are denied him."[15]

The significant phrase in this passage is *harei hu b'ḥezkat me'abed azmo shelo mida'at* ("he is presumed to have taken his life unwittingly"). The *presumption* here is that the person *did in fact take his own life* but that he did so unwittingly. The Geonim and Rishonim who deal with this matter utilize the same term to describe the status of the individual in such a case: "If a person is found strangled and hanging on a tree, he is presumed to have taken his life unwittingly."[16]

It is noteworthy that Maimonides does not use the statement *harei hu b'ḥezkat me'abed azmo shelo mida'at* ("he is presumed to have taken his life unwittingly") with reference to this situation. He indicates that in such a case, *harei zeh b'ḥezkat kol hamaytim* ("it is presumed he [has the same status as] all the other dead [to receive burial rites]").[17] The Geonim and Rishonim appear to concede the fact that the individual took his own life but that he did so unwittingly. There may, however, be situations where there is evidence of intent. Once it is granted that the individual took his own life, there may be grounds to find him culpable in the above circumstances. Maimonides, however, appears to remove the matter completely from the status of suicide and grants the individual the total presumption of innocence.

A rabbinic authority of the eighteenth century in North Africa appears to have chosen the first approach and limits the presumption of innocence to one found strangled in a desolate place, as he may have been killed by others. However, if one was found strangled from the beam in his home, with the door locked, the circumstances point to an intentional suicide.[18]

This view accepts circumstantial evidence as indicative of intention. Despite the absence of statement and witnesses, factors relating to the case are such that it can be adjudicated as an intentional and consequently culpable suicide. A nineteenth-century Ashkenazic authority, however, considers such a situation to be an unintentional suicide. A number of suggestions are given by him as possible causes, i.e., "An evil spirit may have frightened him, or panic took hold of him, or he was frightened that Gentiles would violate him, as was the case with King Saul."[19] Without certain crucial factors, the suicide can never be adjudged as intentional, as the elements to establish culpability are lacking and the presumption of innocence prevails. He thus removes this situation from any culpability and treats the decedent as any deceased, similar to Maimonides' statement, *b'hezkat kol hamaytim* ("it is presumed he [has the same status as] all the other dead").

A nineteenth-century Sephardic authority in Greece extends the viability of the presumption of innocence even further. In his view, one is considered an intentional suicide *only* if he was warned not to take his life.[20] This view evoked sharp rejoinders; it was felt that it actually eliminated the law of an intentional suicide and removed any deterrent elements for potential suicides.[21]

In the nineteenth century, responsa with reference to suicide are quite prevalent. It is possible that this lenient view reflects an attempt to preserve the reputation of the family of the suicide victim. This orientation has its origin in the tannnaitic sources found in *Semahot*.[22] R. Akiba's statement "Leave him to his oblivion," and so forth, and the principle "The public should participate in whatsoever is done out of respect for the living,"[23] are obvious statements of concern for the surviving family. This concern was repeatedly evidenced in the nineteenth-century responsa when suicides became more frequent among Jews.[24]

The intentional suicide, then, falls within very narrow parameters. Evidence of intention must be indubitable. What constitutes *reliable* evidence is the crucial question. The clarification of this is most necessary, because of the presumption of innocence and the concern for the reputation of the surviving family of the suicide victim.

The basic presumption of innocence with regard to suicide is also suggested by the justifiable suicide. There are famous situations in which an individual took his life but did not forfeit the presumption of innocence. Saul's situation is viewed in this light. Naḥmanides and Asheri are of the opinion that Saul was permitted to take his life, and they cite *Genesis Rabbah* 34:13, which excludes Saul from culpability.[25] There is a distinction, however, between the explanation of Naḥmanides and that of Asheri. With regard to Saul, Naḥmanides indicates: *v'khen mazinu be'gadol she'abad azmo lada'at mipnei ha'ones* ("we also find it so in the case of an important person who was compelled to commit suicide"). The term *oness* ("compulsion") is a general one, meaning stress or duress. It seems that Naḥmanides is expanding the permissibility of suicide to cover various areas of difficulty which an individual might face. Asheri, on the other hand, writes with reference to Saul: *v'khen mazinu b'gadol she'abad azmo lada'at mahmat she'mafkirin oto* ("we also find it so in the case of an important person who is made the object of lawless acts"). This is a much more specific delineation of the kind of stress that Saul faced—an anxiety about physical violation and humiliation. Such specificity with regard to the nature of Saul's duress is emphasized by the late Rabbi Kook. He felt that Saul was afraid of the immoral acts which would have been perpetrated against him by the Philistines.[26]

Another kind of permissible suicide is cited by Tosafot *Gittin* 57b, *kafzu*. The Talmud relates that on one occasion, four hundred boys and girls were carried off for immoral purposes. They understood what they were wanted for, jumped into the sea, and drowned. Tosafot in its first explication indicates that the youngsters were afraid of torture, which would have forced them to violate religious tenets. In this view, a suicide to prevent religious transgression, *even though it is only anticipated,* is permissible. In a second view, Tosafot indicates that they would have been tortured intensely; there is no mention of the fear of religious transgression.

The first statement appears to require greater elements of duress for the presumption of innocence to be maintained (i.e., torture leading to anticipated religious transgression). The second view of Tosafot is analogous to Saul's situation, wherein he feared that he would be tortured and humiliated.[27] This view does not require the same degree of duress as the first in order for the presumption of innocence to be applied. R. Meir of Rothenburg speaks of a suicide being justifiable when perpetrated to sanctify God's name. This view clearly maintains the presumption of innocence, because it permits suicide under circumstances of religious persecution.[28]

A well-known scholar of the sixteenth century proposes a novel approach to Saul's situation that has important implications. According to R. Solomon Luria, Saul was concerned that his capture might motivate the Israelites to rescue him. Consequently, many of them would have fallen.[29] Luria says: "When the lives of others are endangered, one can inflict harm upon himself." Saul was *permitted* to do this, as he was acting in his capacity as leader of his people. The kind of motivation involved was the sort which would maintain the presumption of innocence. His motivation for suicide was altruistic and/or protective of his nation's welfare. Luria cites another factor, which also maintains the presumption of innocence. He understands Saul's self-inflicted death as occurring to prevent the desecration of God's name. This desecration would have occurred had Saul, God's anointed, been put to death by the Philistines in a humiliating way. There was a transcendent purpose, then, in Saul's taking his own life.[30]

Luria's understandings as to why Saul's suicide was permissible are quite disparate with regard to their applicability.

His first view can apply to various situations in which individuals, in strategic and responsible assignments, can endanger the lives of others if they are captured. A contemporary rabbinic authority applies Luria's opinion to a contemporary question: Is an Israeli spy captured by the enemy permitted to take his own life? Based on Luria's opinion, he is permitted to do so.[31]

Luria's second opinion would limit the permissibility of suicide to one in a very specific position. It would be relevant to either a king of Israel or a high priest and the like. It is the specific role of the individual which, in Luria's opinion, permits suicide under circumstances of a potential desecration of God's name.[32]

In cases of justifiable suicide, the presumption of innocence remains intact. Factors and circumstances determine whether a particular suicide was permissible. These situations were often perceived as presenting no alternatives except suicide.

A third category of suicide does not relate to the presumption of innocence. It is based on the view stipulated by R. Tam. When one is concerned that due to torture he might violate religious tenets, it is a mitzvah, an obligation, to take one's own life.[33] In this situation, intention is irrelevant, as is permissibility. The individual's higher duty imposes the terrible responsibility of self-destruction.

The material in this chapter demonstrates the following: Intentional suicide was clearly and unequivocally defined in tannaitic sources. Halakhic authorities sought to render their decisions with regard to a suicide within this framework. There were occasions when suicides, while intentional, were considered justifiable. They were perpetrated because of potential abuse and physical humiliation. Halakhic authorities reacted to them with sympathy and on occasion with praise. A noted authority, R. Tam, was of the opinion that under certain circumstances, suicide is actually obligatory.

Chapter 5

Exonerating Circumstances With Regard to Suicide

Suicide as an Act of Repentance

Motivation for suicide was often analyzed in rabbinic literature in terms of its religious acceptability. If the motivation was considered religiously valid, then the suicide was not considered culpable. This is clearly demonstrated with regard to suicide as an act of repentance.

In *Kiddushin* 81b the case of R. Hiyya b. Ashi is cited. He is depicted as having brought about his death, through fasting, due to the guilt he felt with regard to an evil intention. The Talmud accepts this behavior as appropriate religious conduct and does not condemn the fact that he hastened his death through abstention from food.

A similar acceptance of suicide as an act of repentance is found in *Midrash Psalms* 11:7, with regard to Jakum of Zeroroth, the nephew of R. Jose b. Joezer of Zeredah. Jakum taunted his uncle, who was about to be hanged. His uncle in turn retorted: "If it is thus with those who do His will (i.e., that they are to be hanged), how much more with those who anger Him (i.e., individuals like Jakum)." Jakum was filled with remorse and subjected himself to the four modes of execution inflicted by the Beth Din.[1] This was viewed favorably in the Midrash, as indicated by R. Jose's statement, "By a little while he has preceded me into the Garden of Eden."[2]

The situations of R. Ḥiyya b. Ashi and Jakum of Zeroroth are remarkable in that they contradict a basic Jewish tenet—the protection of one's well-being, and the many admonitions against placing oneself in danger.[3]

The situations of R. Ḥiyya b. Ashi and Jakum also appear to be contrary to the passage referring to R. Ḥaninah b. Teradion in *Abodah Zarah* 18a. As he was being burned to death by the Romans, his students told him to open his mouth so that the fire would hasten his death. He replied: "Let Him who gave me (my soul) take it away, but no one should injure himself."

However, the texts of *Kiddushin* 81b and *Midrash Psalms* 11:7 indicate that atonement and repentance are sufficiently powerful religious factors to render such behavior acceptable.

It is not then suicide which is sanctioned; it is the motivation (i.e., repentance) which is deemed religiously significant and acceptable.

I should like to suggest that the cases of R. Ḥiyya b. Ashi and Jakum, on the one hand, and that of R. Ḥaninah b. Teradion, on the other, reflect a specific kind of behavior. Each in his own fashion perpetrated an act of intense piety (*midat ḥasidut*) as he understood it and as his individual needs required. Certainly, R. Ḥiyya's extreme conduct was not necessary to achieve repentance. This could have been accomplished through other means. Jakum's action, too, was not required either to achieve penance or to be reconciled with his uncle, R. Jose. They were filled with remorse to such an extent that one took his life in a very exaggerated fashion (Jakum) and the other brought about death in a slow and painful manner (R. Ḥiyya). In a similiar vein, R. Ḥaninah b. Teradion extended his pain and suffering even though death was inevitable. King Saul's situation was sufficient precedent to allow him to hasten his death. He chose not to, since he felt that an individual should not injure himself. The prolongation of his suffering was then a *personal* act of piety, not necessarily an act governed by specific Judaic precepts.

This act of intense piety (*midat hasidut*) is a unique and highly personal phenomenon. It extends beyond religious requirements. It is difficult to base a halakhic decision only on a precedent which is basically an act of intense personal piety.

This may be reflected in the view of an Ashkenazic authority of the seventeenth century who understood the case of R. Ḥiyya b. Ashi as indicating that one is permitted to take his own life as an act of repentance.[4] However, when adjudicating a case of a man involved in an adulterous relationship who inflicted upon himself the four modes of execution which a Beth Din can impose, he indicates only that the cases of R. Ḥiyya b. Ashi and Jakum of Zeroroth are proof that an individual who committed suicide as an act of repentance is not categorized as an intentional suicide.[5] He is obviously more cautious in applying the situation of R. Ḥiyya b. Ashi to an actual case because it was primarily a *midat ḥasidut,* and he does not say anything in his halakhic decision as to whether the act was permissible.

Rabbi S. Yaffe negates the idea of suicide as an act of repentance and considers it to be sinful. His opinion is that it is incumbent on the individual to protect his life and welfare; suicide is the very antithesis of this. In this view the *midat ḥasidut* cited above is not even considered meritorious.[6]

In another vein, repentance is seen as vitiating any penalty which might accrue as a result of a suicide attempt. Ashkenazic authorities in nineteenth-century Poland and Hungary and a Sephardic authority in Salonika permitted full mourning rites for an individual who, prior to expiring, expressed the wish to repent for taking his own life.[7]

Repentance as motivation for suicide or repentance prior to death for the act of suicide renders the victim inculpable.

Suicide Under Conditions of Incarceration

Does the presumption of innocence prevail with regard to a suicide committed under conditions of incarceration? Are there exonerating factors which would uphold this presumption? What are the precedents, if any, which would help maintain it? Azulai in the eighteenth century wrote that the presumption of innocence should remain intact in the following case: A person imprisoned alone in a governmental cell was found strangled. Although it was unlikely that anyone had strangled him, as he was the sole person in his cell, there was an exonerating factor to be considered. The individual was afraid that he would be tortured by the civil authorities. King Saul is considered the precedent for one who took his life because he was afraid of torture.[8] This is a remarkable and far-reaching application. Saul's suicide occurred at a time of battle and had about it an element of self-sacrifice.[9] The situation here is in no way similar. However, since the aspect of duress is the same (i.e., fear of torture), the application of Saul's case is possible. Another aspect of this case is the fact that the suicide victim knew that he was to be executed by the civil authorities. I should like to suggest that here, too, there is a similarity in that Saul also knew that he would be slain and consequently took his own life.

A later Ashkenazic authority determined that *Kaddish* should be recited for one found hanged in prison. He indicates an exonerating factor similar to that cited above and sees Saul's case as a valid precedent. He views this incident as occurring at a time of great duress, wherein a person is not held accountable for what he does.[10] Incarceration is undoubtedly a condition which maximizes an individual's vulnerability; one's behavior at that time is frequently irrational. A suicide committed under conditions of incarceration is inculpable, and the presumption of innocence is maintained.

Suicide as a Consequence of Poverty

If a suicide is committed due to a person's impoverished state, is this considered a sufficiently extenuating circumstance to remove the onus of culpability from him? Can the presumption of innocence be maintained in such a situation?

An extreme position is taken in *Besamim Rosh*, a work attributed to Asheri by R. Saul Berlin, who wrote a commentary on this text. The presumption of innocence is extended to one in a poverty-stricken state who clearly said, in the presence of two witnesses, that he was disgusted with life and then killed himself. The text indicates that one who takes his life because of intolerable difficulties is not transgressing any prohibition and is actually preventing himself from sinning.

> But one who is in such an unbearable state and more so, that [the act of killing himself] will protect him from sinning, as all of man's troubles, oppressions, and misfortunes turn him against his own benefit and against the will of his Creator; [in such a case] *there is no doubt that such [a suicide] is not forbidden.*

In this opinion the presumption of innocence is so powerful that it overrides a situation which appears to have many aspects of an intentional suicide, i.e., a statement of intention and the presence of witnesses. King Saul is viewed here as a valid precedent for this situation.

The author explains that the true intentional suicide is one whose intellectual orientation negates the physical life in this world and sees the soul as reaching its highest state when it takes leave of the body.[11] It would appear from his analysis that the presumption of innocence is universally applied to all other cases of suicide.

Some of the author's contemporaries were vehemently opposed to this view and questioned the authenticity and authority of the work.[12]

In R. Solomon Kluger's view, poverty does not present sufficient stress to justify taking one's own life and does not fall within the legitimate boundaries of reasonable duress.[13] R. Moses Schreiber also objects to the view cited in the *Besamim Rosh*. He cites the case of R. Ḥaninah b. Teradion as an indication that even if one experiences great difficulties, he should not take his own life. One who does so intentionally is considered a murderer.[14] Both R. Kluger and R. Schreiber were undoubtedly concerned as to the practical implications of the decision stated in the *Besamim Rosh*, as it actually sanctions suicide under conditions of poverty.[15]

A similar question was posed to R. Shalom Schwadron with reference to individuals whose station in life had deteriorated. In order to be free of anguish, poverty, and disgrace, they took their lives. R. Schwadron indicates that no rites are to be denied them.[16]

J. M. Tuktzinski, a contemporary authority, concludes that in spite of the innate weakness of the position of the *Besamim Rosh*, it can still be utilized in determining the status of the individual who took his own life when this view is combined with another possible cause for the suicide.[17]

Poverty, to many authorities, is not the sort of duress which frees an act of suicide from culpability. Those, however, who accept the view presented in the *Besamim Rosh* feel that the duress posed by poverty is of such intensity that the individual should not be considered an intentional suicide.

It would appear that these authorities view the case of Saul as a model of inculpability in suicides committed under duress of any kind.

Humiliation as a Cause of Suicide

The matter of subjective reaction and its relationship to suicide is indicated most poignantly and pointedly in situations of suicides caused by humiliation. What might be a matter of discomfiture or inconvenience to one individual may be psychologically a most threatening event to another. In *Hullin* 94a there are cautions against certain social and business procedures categorized as deceptive practices (*g'neivat da'at*).

An example with very unfortunate consequences is cited.

> A man should not send his neighbor a barrel of wine with oil floating at the mouth of it. It once happened that a man sent his friend a barrel of wine, and there was oil floating at the mouth of the barrel. He went and invited some guests to partake of it, and when they came and he found that it was only wine, he went and hanged himself.

There is no comment about the suicide; it is seen as tragic evidence of what can happen when deception is practiced. It is noteworthy that the suicide is not responded to in a halakhic vein at all.[18] The impact made by this incident was so great that the Talmud saw fit to formulate the admonition cited above.

Another incident of suicide which occurred as a result of intense subjective humiliation is then cited in *Ḥullin* 94a.

> The guests may not give from what is set before them to the son or daughter of the host unless they have the host's permission to do so. It once happened that a man in time of scarcity invited three guests to his house, and he had only three eggs to set before them. When the child of the host entered, one of the guests took his portion and gave it to him. The second guest did likewise, and so did the third. When the father of the child came and saw him stuffing one egg in his mouth and holding two in his hands, he [in rage] knocked him to the ground so that he died. When the child's mother saw this, she went up to the roof and threw herself down and died. He, too, went up to the roof and threw himself down and died.[19]

There is no application of halakhah to the suicides even though a few people were involved and the suicides occurred in a fashion more analogous to the situation in *Semaḥot* (i.e., publicly) than the previous incident cited. The trauma of the multiple suicides was such, however, that here too a principle of social relations was derived from the occurrence.

The trauma of suicide led not only to the promulgation of principles of social behavior, but also contributed to the establishment of a halakhah.

In *Berakoth* 23a there is a discussion of what should be done with phylacteries when one enters a privy. A lesson is drawn from the case of a student who left his tefillin in a hole adjoining the public way. A harlot took them, came to the Beth HaMidrash, and said, "See what so-and-so gave me for my hire." The student's sense of shame and embarrassment was so intense that "he went to the top of a roof, threw himself down, and killed himself." The Talmud states, "Thereupon, they ordained that a man should hold them in his garment and in his hand, and then go in."

The decision with reference to the phylacteries was obviously not a preferred one, as it involves a possible degradation of them. The suicide apparently made such an intense impression that in consequence of it this difficulty was overlooked and the halakhah was instituted accordingly.

It is conceivable that these suicides are not discussed because our Sages did not want to draw attention to them, so as not to popularize these tragic incidents. Perhaps they deemed the lack of discussion to be a preventive measure with regard to suicide.

There is a tone of empathy in the Talmud with regard to all the incidents mentioned in this section. The Talmud accepts without comment the tragic subjective reactions of individuals who considered themselves humiliated and disgraced. I suggest that the direction of the passages mentioned in this section would lead to a lenient decision with regard to one who took his own life as a result of subjective humiliation.

The decision of R. Shalom Schwadron cited above demonstrates the viability of this assumption. He exonerates one who took his life because of a subjective feeling of humiliation due to a deterioration of his position in life.[20]

An individual who was involved in a duel because he was embarrassed and humiliated by someone and was killed would not be considered a culpable suicide.[21] This would, in my opinion, fall under the generally lenient tendency extended to suicides committed due to humiliation and chagrin.

Suicide and the Consumption of Alcohol

Self-induced intoxication is not usually considered an exonerating factor in legal matters. As the Tosefta (*Terumot* 3:1) indicates: *shikor harei hu k'pikeiyakh l'khol davar* ("a drunkard in every case is to be considered as one who is in total possession of his faculties"). Can a suicide committed while the individual is under the influence of alcohol be considered inculpable? Rabbi H. Medini, a Sephardic authority of the nineteenth century, understood the inculpability of a suicide due to the consumption of alcohol in terms of the extent of the distortion of the individual's perception.

In his view, the determination of a case of suicide as a result of inebriation is similar to the status of the inebriated individual in other situations indicated by the Talmud in *Erubin* 65a.

"The sale or purchase of an intoxicated person is valid. If he committed a transgression involving the penalty of death, he is to be executed." This passage in the Talmud concludes with R. Ḥanina's statement: "This applies only to one who did not reach the stage of Lot's drunkenness, but one who did reach such a stage is exempt from all responsibilities."[22] According to this view, if the individual took his life in a state wherein his perception was not totally distorted, the suicide would be culpable. If his inebriation reached an extreme state in which his perception was totally distorted, he is considered inculpable.

A Sephardic authority of the nineteenth century made allowances for an individual whose inebriation was not a constant factor of his personality but was experienced periodically. During one of these periods of inebriation he drank poison. After his state of inebriation waned, he said that he had drunk poison and requested that medical aid be given him. The doctor's efforts did not help, however, and the individual died that same day.

The following solution was proposed:

> Individuals who are familiar with his situation should be questioned. If in most instances his inebriation reached that of Lot's, then it should be determined that at this particular time too, he reached that state, and the law of the intentional suicide does not apply to him.
>
> If in most instances he did not become inebriated to that extent [of Lot], we can determine that now, too, he did not reach that state, and the law of the intentional suicide *does* apply to him, and consequently even the *Kaddish* should not be said for him.[23]

The issue is whether a presumption of innocence can be maintained if the individual took his life while under the influence of alcohol. The primary consideration is the degree to which alcohol hampered his functioning. I should like to suggest that this has relevance to a contemporary situation—the consumption of drugs. If the consumption is so substantial that an individual's perception is totally distorted and he cannot function properly, his suicide would be deemed inculpable.

Suicide and Its Relationship to Mental Illness

Evidence of mental illness eliminates any possible presumption of intention in cases of suicide, since the suicide is not the result of a responsible decision. R. Yitzchak Lampronti indicates this in *Paḥad Yizhak*.

An individual who had periods of lucidity and periods of insanity took his life by jumping out of the window. It was determined that at the time he jumped he was insane, and therefore all mourning rites were to be observed for him.[24]

Rabbi J. M. Epstein in *Arukh ha-Shulḥan* goes even further and indicates that the suicide itself is proof of the mental imbalance suffered by the individual. As he says: "It is truly a farfetched matter that a person should perpetrate such a heinous deed with a lucid mind."[25]

This is quite similar to the view in contemporary psychiatric thought with reference to suicide. Dr. George Murphy has written: "The descriptive facts are that most persons who commit suicide are suffering from clinically recognizable psychiatric illnesses."[26]

Mental illness, then, makes the question of intent irrelevant. In many instances the suicide attempt is in and of itself an indication that the individual is mentally ill and consequently not responsible for his actions. The suicidal act, then, is outside the scope of culpability when the person has evidenced symptoms of mental disease.

Suicide Resulting from Identification with a Person or Situation

There are instances cited in talmudic literature where acts of suicide were perpetrated due to the individual's identification with someone who had died or with a particular situation. An instance of this is the case of the launderer who was absent on the day that Rabbi[27] died.

> On the day that Rabbi died a *bat kol* went forth and announced, "Whosoever has been present at the death of Rabbi is destined to enjoy the life of the world-to-come." A certain launderer who used to come to him every day failed to call on that day; as soon as he heard this he went on a roof, fell to the ground, and died. A *bat kol* came forth and announced: "That launderer also is destined to enjoy the life of the world-to-come."[28]

This passage can be understood in two ways. The launderer was granted a share in the world-to-come despite his suicidal act.[29] This reward was granted him because his devotion to Rabbi's memory was so sincere and the remorse he felt at possibly forfeiting his share in the world-to-come so intense that even his suicide did not deter him from the privilege that was his. This perhaps is the reason for the indication of the *bat kol*. Without it the launderer would not have been granted a share in the world-to-come.

The passage can also be understood as indicating that he merited a share in the world-to-come *because* his suicide demonstrated the intensity of his attachment to Rabbi and his remorse at possibly forfeiting a share in the world-to-come.[30]

It is my view that it is the latter explanation which applies to this case. There is, however, an important qualification. The suicide combined with other factors assured the launderer a share in the world-to-come. In this case the launderer's anguish over Rabbi's death, in addition to his suicide, granted him a share in the world-to-come. The suicide, then, was proof of the intensity of his feelings.

Another such instance is related in *Abodah Zarah* 18a. The passage refers to R. Ḥaninah b. Teradion, who was immolated by the Romans for studying Torah in defiance of the prohibition which they had issued. His disciples urged him to "open then thy mouth so that the fire enter into thee." He replied, "Let Him who gave me [my soul] take it away, but no one should injure himself." The executioner than said to him:

"Rabbi, if I raise the flame and take away the tufts of wool from over thy heart, will thou cause me to enter into the life to come?" "Yes," he replied. "Then swear unto me [he urged]." He swore unto him. He thereupon raised the flame and removed the tufts of wool from over his heart, and his soul departed speedily. The executioner then jumped and threw himself into the fire. And a *bat kol* exclaimed, "R. Ḥaninah b. Teradion and the executioner have been assigned to the world-to-come." When Rabbi heard it, he wept and said. "One may acquire eternal life in a single hour, another after many years."

It would be inappropriate here to claim that the executioner was granted a share in the world-to-come despite his suicide. The text of the Talmud indicates that "R. Ḥaninah b. Teradion and the executioner have been assigned to the world-to-come." R. Ḥaninah's death did not involve suicide at all, and his reward as well as the executioner's was a share in the world-to-come. Here, too, the executioner's suicide, resulting from his identification with R. Ḥaninah's plight, combined with the empathy he showed R. Ḥaninah, assured him a spiritual reward.[31]

A suicide which resulted from identification with persons who died is mentioned in 2 Maccabees 7 and *Gittin* 57b. In the apocryphal account, Antiochus is described as putting a mother's seven sons to death because they refused to bow to an idol. There is no clear indication that the mother committed suicide. In *Gittin* 57b the woman is depicted as throwing herself to her death after witnessing the murder of her sons by the emperor for refusing to bow to the idol. The Talmud obviously approves, as it concludes the passage with the verse "a joyful mother of children."[32]

Another incident of suicide by a non-Jew because of identification with a Sage of Israel involves R. Gamaliel.

R. Gamaliel was in hiding, to elude the Romans. A Roman officer went up secretly to him and said, "If I save you, will you bring me into the world-to-come?" He replied, "Yes." He then asked him, "Will you swear it unto me?" And the latter took an oath. The officer then mounted the roof and threw himself down and died. There was a tradition (among the Romans)[33] that when a decree is made and one of their own (leaders) dies, then that decree is voided. "Thereupon a Voice from Heaven was heard, declaring, 'This high officer is destined to enter into the world-to-come.' "[34]

In this situation the suicide was clearly the reason for the spiritual reward, as it was the cause for the decree to be annulled. There is a distinct note of approval associated with it.

This passage is followed by one in which suicide is viewed as a final act of identification with tragedy and defeat.[35]

> Our Rabbis have taught when the First Temple was about to be destroyed, bands upon bands of young priests with the keys of the Temple in their hands assembled and mounted the roof of the Temple and exclaimed, "Master of the Universe, as we did not have the merit to be faithful treasurers, these keys are handed back into Thy keeping." They then threw the keys up towards heaven. And there emerged the figure of a hand and received the keys from them. Whereupon they jumped and fell into the fire. It is in allusion to them that the prophet Isaiah laments, "The burden concerning the Valley of Vision. What aileth thee now, that thou art wholly gone up the housetops; thou that are full of uproar, a tumultuous city, a joyous town? Thy slain are not slain with the sword, nor dead in battle."[36]

The Talmud speaks of the passage which describes the incident in a spirit of resignation and acceptance, and sees in the action of the young priests the fulfillment of Isaiah's prophecy. There is a tone of approval in the description of their act.

The incidents described above indicate that a suicide committed as a result of identification with one who has died is not considered culpable. The same is true if a suicide occurs as a result of identification with a tragic situation.

Chapter 6

Suicide as an Act of Martyrdom

This chapter deals only with suicide as an act of martyrdom, i.e., when one kills oneself to avoid transgressing a religious precept, and not when one allows oneself to be killed so as not to transgress a religious precept. Of particular significance is whether the prohibition against suicide in Genesis 9:5 also applied to a suicide committed as an act of martyrdom.

No explicit case of a suicide committed as an act of martyrdom is mentioned in the Bible. King Saul is the paradigm which many authorities utilize for a suicide committed under stress, and this has application to situations far different from his.[1] There are those, however, who view his death as constituting a suicide as an act of martyrdom.

R. Isaac of Corbeil sees Saul's mode of death as an appropriate example for situations involving martyrdom. "Those martyrs who killed themselves because they did not feel that they could stand the trial are considered completely righteous, and the proof of this is Saul."[2]

His reference to those suicides as *kedoshim* ("martyrs") is a clear indication that he approves of their action and that he sees Saul's death as an act of martyrdom. Likewise R. Meir of Rothenburg indicates that suicide, as an act of martyrdom, is a permitted deed, and brings proof for this view from Saul's situation and from the incident of the four hundred boys and girls who were imprisoned by the Romans (*Gittin* 57b).[3]

Rabbi A. I. Kook conjectures that Saul feared that he would be abused in an immoral fashion and that he would be publicly abused in order to bring shame on the faith of Israel.[4] This constituted an attempt to force him to transgress religious teachings. His suicide, then, was an act of martyrdom.

However, many authorities view Saul's suicide as being a reaction to an untenable situation.[5]

Suicide as an act of martyrdom is not mentioned in the Mishnah and Tosefta.

According to Josephus, the defenders of Masada, the last outpost of the Jewish war against Rome, perished through a mass suicide.[6]

A crucial question with regard to Masada is the appropriateness within the Judaic tradition of the act of mass suicide that according to Josephus' account took place there.[7] Rabbinic sources contemporaneous with the incidents at Masada do not respond to the events that occurred there.

Passages in *Sanhedrin* 74a–b and P.T. Sheviit 4:2 discuss the circumstances making it incumbent on an individual to undergo martyrdom. The phrase used in the above sugyot is *yehareg v'al ya'avor* ("letting oneself be killed rather than sin"). The word *yehareg* indicates one being killed by someone else. These passages do not indicate that suicide is mandated. This is further evidenced by the fact that with the exception of very few authorities, there is no association of the martyrdom mentioned in this sugya with suicide.[8]

An aggadic section in *Gittin* 57b describes a mass suicide by drowning, which is a significant model of suicide, as an act of martyrdom.

> On one occasion four hundred boys and girls were carried off for immoral purposes. They divined what they were wanted for and said to themselves, "If we drown in the sea we shall attain the life of the future world." The eldest among them expounded the verse "The Lord said, I will bring again from Bashan, I will bring again from the depths of the sea" (Psalm 68:23). "I will bring again from Bashan"—from between the lion's teeth.[9] "I will bring again from the depths of the sea"—those who drown in the sea. When the girls heard this they all leaped into the sea. The boys then drew the moral for themselves, saying, "If these for whom this is natural act so, shall not we for whom it is

unnatural?" They also leaped into the sea. Of them the text says, "Yea, for thy sake we are killed all the day long; we are counted as sheep for the slaughter" (Psalm 44:23).

This passage contains some interesting problems.

1. Their possible involvement in sin was not immediate, i.e., no one was threatening or demanding that they do immoral acts at the moment they decided to take their lives.
2. They appeared to have some hesitation as to whether their act would be considered meritorious, as indicated by their discussion prior to their drowning themselves.

It is possible that their hesitation was due to doubts as to whether their impending suicide would be considered an acceptable act. The Talmud obviously considers their act as meritorious and praiseworthy, and deems it an act of supreme service to the Almighty, i.e., "For Thy sake we are killed all the day long."[10]

R. Tam considers the taking of one's own life to avoid transgressing a religious teaching to be a mitzvah. In Tosafot *Abodah Zarah* 18a, s.v. *V'al*, he clearly indicates that where one is afraid that idol worshipers will cause him to sin through unbearable torture, it is a duty to hurt oneself (i.e., take one's own life). This is the case in *Gittin* 57b with regard to the children taken for sinful purposes who cast themselves into the sea. It is interesting that R. Tam did not cite the case of Saul as proof for his view. I suggest that he did not consider Saul's suicide as an act of martyrdom. In his view, it was a reaction to an untenable situation which had become unendurably stressful.

R. Tam does not limit his opinion to any particular sins which one may face. While the proof he cites deals with immorality (i.e., the case of the four hundred boys and girls in *Gittin* 57b), his view might very well apply to other situations too. It is significant that he does not classify this as a situation to be characterized by the requirement *yehareg v'al ya'avor* ("letting oneself be killed rather than sin"). This is an indication that he does not necessarily consider suicide to be mandated in those situations wherein martyrdom was required.

Historical and poetic texts are replete with laudatory descriptions of those who took their own lives to avoid transgressing religious precepts. Historical evidence points to the advocacy of this by certain leaders of the communities involved.

In France in 1007 C.E. under King Robert II, an attempt was made to convert the Jews by force. Some women who were witnesses to this decided to drown themselves. They are referred to as "precious women," *nashim y'karot*.[11]

In 1096 during the First Crusade, there were incidents of suicide as acts of martyrdom in Speyer, Worms, Mainz, and Xanten. R. Solomon b. Samson reports these acts as praiseworthy.[12]

During the Second Crusade (1146) an incident which can be understood as constituting a suicide as an act of martyrdom is mentioned in *Emek ha-Bakha* of R. Joseph ha-Kohen.[13]

An incident of mass suicide in York, England, in 1191, initiated by R. Yom Tov, is described in *Emek ha-Bakha*. The text praises these incidents.[14]

In Erfurt (1221) the Jews were accused of stealing a Gentile child in order to kill him and drink his blood. This led to many Jews being put to death. Some chose suicide as a means of escape.

The "Memorbuch" which memorializes the martyrs of Erfurt reads as follows:

> The martyrs of Erfurt in 1221, on the 25th day of Sivan were the following: R. Samuel Ḥazan b. R. Kalonymus and his wife Hannah; R. Joel the Pious, and with him his wife, Sloyda; R. Shem-Tov Halevi, who committed suicide in front of the Holy Ark; R. Mordecai b. R. Elyakim Halevi; R. Joseph b. R. Samuel; R. Isaac; R. Moses and his two maiden daughters, Madrona and Rachel [who] threw themselves into the fire. R. Kalonymus and his wife, the young man, R. Zeligman and another young man, R. Shabbetai, his wife and daughter; and the lad Joseph threw himself into the fire. R. Kalonymus and his daughter.[15]

The *kinot* written to commemorate this tragedy speak of them as acts of sacrifice to the Almighty, deserving of a response by Him. The suicides are viewed as sacred acts, which sanctify God's name.

The Levite exults before You,
He stuck out his neck and was slaughtered for You,
Joseph and his offspring rejoiced and obeyed You,
And now, our Lord, the King, the eyes of Israel are all upon You.

Moses, Your chosen one, publicly sanctified Your Name,
His son and daughter together ran into the flame.
Two martyred sisters plunged into the fire without fear,
The Lord became known as King, and His name was One.

Why are You silent, my King and Holy One?
That upon these You restrained Yourself and did not take the lead
Pure-hearted ones were transported [to their deaths] for naught
If the King would be so kind, to give me my life.[16]

In 1298 the Jews were accused of desecrating a sacramental wafer. During the Rindfleisch persecutions[17] there were many instances of suicide to avert massacre, destruction, and conversion. They are responded to with praise and empathy. The poet describes the martyred suicides as a magnificent demonstrations of loyalty to the Almighty.

I am distressed and embittered for you, glorious Rothenburg,
My heart has ceased to rejoice, and all happiness and joy have passed by.
He who dwells with them observed a great, mighty wonder.
My children walking into the flames with songs and dance;
To profess the unity and sanctity of their Creator and His exalted Name.
Merciful women held their children to their hearts in confusion.
She is brought forward, her child tied to her, and the bond remains unbroken.
The nubile maiden, daughter of my people,
Kindled the flames and plunged upon it and fell [to her death].

The martyrdom of the women of Nuremberg is described poignantly.

> Beautiful women caused their children to writhe in pain, cleaving them
> With vigor and groans; each woman unique in her piety
> She slaughtered and slaughtered, arranged her sacrifice
> In a single day she slaughtered herself and her child.[18]

In 1320, during the Shepherd's Edict (*G'zerat ha-Ro'im*), there were many suicides. These were responded to without criticism or negation in the historical works which described them.[19]

During the Black Plague (1348), incidents of suicide were related, sometimes accompanied by wondrous results.[20] Concerning the massacres in Prague (1389), a prominent rabbinic leader wrote of the selflessness of the martyrs.

> The edict struck the metropolis of Prague
> In the year 5149 after the Creation.
> The righteous fell before the wicked, and justice miscarried.
> How the mighty staff is shattered, the magnificent staff . . .
> [Even] the weakhearted slays his son!
>
> A mother's compassion for her son did not allow him to escape!
> [These were] sacrifices from all who would offer;
> Whether male or female, they would be sacrificed while still pure.
> A venerable teacher acclaimed by his flock,
> In order that he not be mistreated, hastened
> To slaughter his children and other members of his family, together with himself.
> For this my heart trembles and is moved.[21]

In fourteenth-century Spain there were many suicides as acts of martyrdom.

Hasdai Crescas, reporting about the persecutions in that country in 5151 (1391), speaks of suicides in Toledo and Barcelona. In Toledo, descendants of R. Asher took their lives.[22] In Barcelona, Crescas' son was killed, and many committed suicide to sanctify God's name.[23]

Incidents of suicide among the Jews in Portugal are related by R. Elijah Kapsali in this manner:

> They decided to throw themselves into wells, ditches, and caves, lest they enter into broken wells [i.e., apostasy or immorality]. Many did so, [showing their] contempt [of their tormentors], and their corpses were like refuse on the streets with no one to bury them.[24]

R. Judah b. Isaac Abrabanel, in a poem written to commemorate the expulsion from Spain and Portugal, writes of the suicides committed to avoid transgressing religious principles.

> And many committed suicide, lest
> They transgress the Torah of the Lord, to my desolation.[25]

During the massacres of 1647 and 1648 (*g'zerot 'taḥ v'tat*), instances of martyred suicides were reported by Nathan Hannover. Hannover's description is found in his work *Yeven M'zulah*. He cites some incidents that occurred in the city of Nemirov.[26]

In 1768 in Uman (Ukraine) some Jews responded to the pogroms perpetrated against them by Catherine II by taking their lives.[27]

The continued affirmative response to suicide as an act of martyrdom is demonstrated in contemporary times by the late Ashkenazic Chief Rabbi of Israel, Rabbi I. Unterman. He indicates with reference to those who martyred themselves that "their merit [*z'khut*] remains forever, and their memory is sacred for all generations, and none can stand in their domain."[28]

The one exception to the very affirmative stance taken by rabbinic authorities, historians, poets, and liturgists with regard to suicide as an act of martyrdom is the position of R. Solomon Luria. He prohibits one from actively inflicting harm upon oneself. He states that even if one is captured by Gentiles and is

afraid that he will be forced to worship other gods, he still must
not take his own life. In Luria's view, a concomitant of this is
that one is not allowed to take the lives of one's children during
a time of religious persecution. "Since one is not even allowed
to kill himself, surely he cannot murder others." However, he
does permit a passive suicide during a time of religious persecution. "Still, one is permitted to set the house ablaze during a
persecution so that he and his family burn to death. This is not
considered suicide, but it is as if he let himself be killed, which is
permissible [in Jewish law]."[29]

His opposition to active suicide is because one is not permitted to inflict harm upon oneself. This view is based on that of
R. Isaac (Ri) in Tosafot *Bava Kamma* 9lb, s.v. *ela,* who indicates,
she'asur laḥbol afilu l'zorekh ("that it is forbidden to inflict harm
on oneself even when there is a need").[30] However, in a case of
passive suicide, this is obviated.

In tracing suicide as an act of martyrdom through the
sources, frequent episodes of martyred suicides are found.
These occurred either as the response to threatened conversion or to intense persecution. In either case they were not
condemned, and Genesis 9:5 is not considered as prohibiting
these incidents. During the medieval period, these acts were
considered a *kiddush hashem* and were described as such in
liturgical and poetic literature. R. Tam's dictum that one should
take his own life if he was afraid that he would be forced to
transgress religious principles gives sanction and approval to
this behavior.[31] In addition, Christianity was considered by
many to be tantamount to idolatry,[32] and while *yehareg v'al
ya'avor* ("letting oneself be killed rather than sin") did not
mandate suicide, many took it upon themselves to take their
own lives, since it was not disallowed by explicit prohibition in
the Torah. Even Luria, who prohibits active suicide, permits a
passive suicide in time of persecution, such as burning the
house over oneself.

The principle that one can take one's life if one is afraid of
torture which will cause him to transgress religious tenets is
stated by Tosafot *Gittin* 57b, s.v. *kafzu.* This undoubtedly gave

sanction to the suicides which occurred as a result of forced conversion and persecution.

The absence of sources would indicate that during the Moslem period, mass suicides among Jews do not seem to have occurred.

It is most significant that in the Holocaust period there is an opinion which viewed suicide conversely as a *hillul hashem* ("blasphemy").[33] Suicides during that period would, in this view, have demonstrated that the Jews had no trust in the mercy of God. They also would have signified surrender to the Nazis and the success of their evil designs. Those Jews who were least assimilated had the lowest suicide rates during that tragic epoch of Jewish history.[34]

The question of suicide as an act of martyrdom is debated by two contemporary authorities, Rabbi S. Goren, the former Ashkenazic Chief Rabbi of Israel, and Rabbi Moshe Neriah. R. Goren's understanding of King Saul's situation and the events of Masada served as the basis for one of his conclusions. R. Neriah differs with him and cites authorities who, in his opinion, either prohibit or at most permit suicide as an act of martyrdom. R. Neriah emphasizes that the period of the Holocaust clearly demonstrates that suicide under those circumstances would not have been an acceptable reaction.

R. Goren states as follows:

> When one's capture by the enemy would bring about a *hillul hashem* [blasphemy] and would allow the enemy to glorify itself thereby, yet at the end of the matter they would still kill him it is an obligation [mitzvah] to commit suicide, rather than fall into the hands of the enemy, as we find in the case of King Saul and the people of Masada.[35]

Rabbi M. Neriah takes him to task in a sharp rebuttal. He points to the Ri and R. Solomon Luria, who prohibit actively taking one's own life under any circumstances, and to Naḥmanides, who at most permits suicide under conditions of duress but certainly does not consider it an obligation at any time. He indicates, too, that there are other sources which seem

to modify R. Tam's strong position. R. Neriah points to the
period of the Holocaust in vigorously rejecting R. Goren's view.

> Our brethren who were placed in jeopardy and were incarcer-
> ated in the ghettos and the death camps, and were readied for
> torture and for abrogation of the Faith. If they had conducted
> themselves according to R. Goren's decision, not one of them
> would have remained. This, then, is a decision which is both
> mistaken and dangerous, and one should keep himself from it
> because the Giver of the Torah commanded us to live: "And you
> shall live by them, and not die by them."[36]

The sources clearly indicate that suicide as an act of martyrdom, while not mandated, was invariably considered a meritorious deed. In my view, there is no overwhelming evidence that
an individual must actively take his life under any circumstances. Even R. Tam's citation of the aggadic section in *Gittin*
57b would appear to place such behavior in the category of
desirable conduct more than in that of obligatory behavior.
This is further substantiated by the fact that he does not place
suicide as an act of martyrdom in the category of *yehareg v'al
ya'avor.* There is no question, however, that when suicide as an
act of martyrdom did take place, it was considered a *kiddush
hashem* of the highest order.

Chapter 7

Conclusions

Although suicide is viewed with the utmost severity by many authorities and often spoken of in the most condemnatory terms,[1] there is no explicit statement in the Torah prohibiting it. The halakhic statement which enjoins against it is that of the Tanna R. Eleazar, quoted in a discussion of *Baba Kamma* 9lb. This enjoinder, based on Genesis 9:5, is *v'akh et dimkhem l'nafshoteikhem edrosh* ("and surely your blood of your lives will I require"). R. Eleazar is quoted as saying: *Miyad nafshoteikhem edrosh et dimkhem* ("I will require your blood if taken by your hands"). R. Eleazar's statement is brought into the talmudic discussion peripherally and is not commented upon either in agreement or disagreement.[2]

The Targumim do not take cognizance of R. Eleazar's statement. In their translations they do not explain Genesis 9:5 as relating to suicide.

A source that demonstrates the acceptance of R. Eleazar's view by removing the onus of suicide from King Saul, Hananiah, Mishael, and Azariah is *Genesis Rabbah* 34:13: *v'akh et dimkhem l'nafshoteikhem edrosh* ("and surely the blood of your lives will I require"). The Midrash asks whether this is applicable to Saul's situation. *Yakhol k'Saul, talmud lomar "akh"*. The word *akh* surely excludes Saul from culpability as a suicide. *Yakhol k'Hananiah, Mishael v'Azariah, talmud lomar "akh"* ("it might be said that it is like [the case of] Hananiah, Mishael, and Azariah, so [the Torah] teaches us 'surely' "). Here, too, the word *akh* ("surely") excludes Hananiah, Mishael, and Azariah from culpability.

The fact, however, that the prohibition is not explicit led to substantial differences in the interpretation of this verse (Gen. 9:5) by biblical commentators.

The biblical exegetes who dealt with this verse are divided into three categories: the commentators who accept the talmudic explanation as the actual meaning of the verse,[3] those who offer their own interpretation but cite the rabbinic interpretation as well,[4] and those who reject the rabbinic interpretation or do not mention it at all.[5]

The suicides mentioned in the Bible are Samson, Saul, and Ahithophel. Samson's death is not responded to as a suicide, either in rabbinic sources or in biblical exegetical literature. His death is viewed as resulting from an act of warfare, which brought about the destruction of the enemy.

Saul's death, however, gives rise to much discussion and analysis. Most of the talmudic and midrashic sources dealing with the events relating to Saul's death are concerned with the aspect of its predetermination. In spite of the fact that Genesis 34:13 exonerates Saul's behavior from culpability, biblical commentators had difficulty in accepting Saul's suicide and sought to explain it in varying ways. Saadia Gaon claims that the Amalekite killed him.[6] Kimḥi at first says that the Amalekite killed him. In his alternative interpretation, Kimḥi grants that Saul took his own life, since his death was predetermined, and because his situation had become intolerable.[7] Abrabanel favors the version that the Amalekite killed him.[8] The interpretations are stated despite the fact that Saul is expressly exonerated in *Genesis Rabbah*   34:13, and the Book of Chronicles does not state the incident of the Amalekite at all.[9] To the commentators, then, the prohibition with regard to suicide had the force of an explicit one, and their attempts at resolving Saul's situation are evidence of this. Nonetheless, Saul is the prototype of the suicide committed under conditions of great stress, and as such becomes a standard by which other suicides are judged.

Ahithophel's suicide contains elements of predetermination too. It was also seen by some commentators as the final act of a desperate man who was afraid of political and economic vengeance.[10]

The tannaitic sources in *Semaḥot* define the intentional suicide and delineate the mourning rites for one who has been thus characterized. The determination is that a culpable suicide, subject to halakhic penalties, is one carried out through responsible choice with intent definitely stated by the perpetrator and witnessed by others.

If the individual is adjudged an intentional suicide, there is no rending of clothes, no baring of shoulders, and no eulogizing for him. However, the people line up for him and the mourner's blessing is recited over him out of respect for the living. This is a clear indication that mourning rites are to honor the deceased. The intentional suicide is not deserving of this honor.

An individual found hanging strangled from a tree or slain impaled upon a sword is presumed to have taken his life unwittingly, and no rites are to be denied him. According to Naḥmanides' interpretation of *Semaḥot* 2:4 and 2:5, inculpability applies in a case of a minor, because a minor is equivalent to an adult acting in an irrational manner.[11] In Asheri's interpretation, the inculpability indicated in these baraitas was due to the irrational and panic-stricken reaction of the adult individuals who took their lives.[12]

Some early authorities stipulated varying kinds of statements and conditions for determining an intentional suicide. This precise definition was necessary because of the presumption of innocence which every person has, including the suicide victim. The viability of the presumption of innocence is demonstrated in the baraita (cited above) that "If an individual is found strangled hanging from a tree or slain impaled upon a sword, he is presumed to have taken his life unwittingly. He is not to be denied any rites."[13]

There are suicides which have been adjudged justifiable. King Saul is the paradigm of this kind of suicide because he took his life under duress. Many halakhic authorities applied Saul's suicide under duress to situations quite dissimilar to the one he faced. R. Solomon Luria sees Saul's case as a special situation and stresses its exclusivity. In his view, other lives would have been endangered, since the Israelites would have perished in battle trying to save their king. Saul was thus permitted to kill himself. In addition, if he had died at the hand of the Philistines, it would have been a desecration of God's Name. Consequently, he was permitted to take his life.[14]

Tosafot considers a justifiable suicide the case of four hundred boys and girls who were carried off for immoral purposes (*Gittin* 57b). Tosafot justifies their suicide with a twofold explanation

1. They feared torture which would have forced them to violate religious principles.
2. They were afraid that their torture would be of an intense nature and of long duration, as they would not have been put to death by their captors.

In either case, the suicide was deemed justifiable, since duress of an extreme nature was involved. R. Tam appears to favor the first explication of Tosafot. In his opinion, if one is concerned that he will transgress religious principles due to torture, it is a mitzvah, an obligation, for him to take his own life.

Halakhic authorities established certain exonerating factors with regard to suicide. If the motivation for suicide was deemed religiously acceptable, i.e., a suicide committed as an act of repentance, the suicide is not considered culpable. Where social conditions bring about intense fear and anguish, e.g., incarceration, a suicide under such conditions is exonerated.

A substantial debate arose as to whether poverty is an exonerating factor in suicide. Those authorities opposed to accepting poverty as a factor removing culpability from a suicide indicate that poverty is an adversity of life which an individual should tolerate. Those who accept it as a mitigating factor in determining culpability and hence remove the penalty from a suicide are of the view that the crucial element here is the subjective reaction of the individual. The intensity of stress might be such that the individual could not tolerate it, and consequently he is not considered an intentional suicide.

Rabbi J. M. Tuktzinski indicates that the lenient position with regard to poverty may be utilized in determining the status of a suicide when this view is combined with another possible cause.

Suicides committed due to a subjectively perceived humiliation are treated with empathy in the Talmud. The impression given by the Talmud in citing these incidents is that suicides which occur as a result of these reactions should be dealt with leniently.

An individual who is in an inculpable legal state because he is inebriated to the extent that he is completely oblivious to what he is doing is not penalized as an intentional suicide. Where there is an indication of mental illness the individual is not considered to be an intentional suicide, as the basis of the intent itself is pathological. Suicides resulting from identification with a person or situation are described with empathy in the Talmud. Consequently, one who takes his life as a result of this would not be considered culpable.[15]

Suicide as an act of martyrdom is considered praiseworthy and meritorious. This is evident from all the sources which deal with this matter in rabbinic, historical, poetic, and liturgical literature. The evidence is that suicide is not necessarily included as part of the martyrdom discussed in the sugya *yehareg v'al ya'avor* ("letting oneself be killed rather than sin") (*Sanhedrin* 74a–b, P.T. *Sheviit* 4:2). It appears, however, that it was always considered an option when necessity arose. When an individual took his life under these circumstances, it was termed a *kiddush hashem*.[16]

Certain conclusions can be suggested as a result of this study.

1. The culpability of any suicide has been reduced almost to the degree of being nonexistent. This is due to the following reasons:

   a. There is no explicit verse in the Torah prohibiting suicide.

   b. The requirement, established by the tannaitic sources in *Semahot*, that there must be a statement prior to a suicide attempt to establish intention, greatly limits the possibility of culpability.

c. Tannaitic sources in *Semaḥot* associate suicide with irrational behavior (*Semaḥot* 2:4 and 2:5). Some early authorities greatly reduced the extent of a suicide's culpability. They viewed Saul's suicide as inculpable because he took his life under duress (*anus*). This understanding was applied by later authorities to circumstances far different from Saul's. The underlying similarity to Saul's case, in their view, was that the individual took his life under great duress. Consequently, the scope of duress was greatly broadened in later responsa literature, and many additional exonerating elements were cited..

d. All these elements forge a substantial basis for a lenient view with regard to suicide, which would render the suicide inculpable.[17]

2. Judging from its frequency in responsa literature, suicide occurred with some regularity in Jewish communities only since the nineteenth century. Using statistical data, others have arrived at the same conclusion.[18]

3. Suicides as acts of martyrdom were not disallowed by the rabbinic interpretation of Genesis 9:5. Although the sugya of *yehareg v'al ya'avor* ("letting oneself be killed rather than sin") does not mandate suicide, in Christian Europe, at various times, this type of suicide was considered an action of great religious commitment, entirely appropriate and praiseworthy. This attitude was probably due to the fact that forced conversion to Christianity was viewed as tantamount to idolatry.[19] There was sanction for this action in the view of R. Tam.[20]

It is significant that in Moslem lands, mass suicides are nonexistent. Islam was not viewed as *avodah zarah* ("idolatry"). Consequently, martyrdom was not a frequent alternative.[21]

4. The only time that Judaism ever viewed suicide affirmatively was when it was committed as an act of martyrdom. Otherwise it was *never* sanctioned. It may have been considered inculpable due to various exonerating circumstances, but it was never an approved act.[22]

5. There does not appear to be any marked tendency to leniency or stringency vis-à-vis suicide with regard to whether

an authority is Ashkenazic or Sephardic. Certain Ashkenazic authorities have displayed much leniency (R. Moses Schreiber);[23] others have been quite stringent (R. Solomon Kluger).[24] The same can be said of Sephardic authorities. Leniency was indicated by R. Ḥayyim David Azulai,[25] and stringency by R. Aaron Azriel.[26]

6. It is significant that the early association of suicide with irrational behavior which is found in tannaitic sources is a view which psychiatry endorses today. The dominant psychiatric view is that suicide is evidence of mental illness and represents a final act in the disintegration of the personality.[27] This is of great importance to the rabbi, in his determination of a case of suicide, as medical opinion is indicating that the individual is not responsible for his suicidal act and hence should bear no culpability.

7. The direction of the research provides a contemporary rabbi with many elements which would render a suicide inculpable so that the suicide victim should not be denied any rites.

Excursus I

Mourning Procedures for an Intentional Suicide

The tannaitic sources in *Semaḥot* indicate the mourning procedure to be followed for the intentional suicide.

> For a suicide, no rites whatsoever should be observed. . . . There may be no rending of clothes, no baring of shoulders, and no eulogizing for him. But people should line up for him, and the mourner's blessing should be recited over him, out of respect for the living. The general rule is: the public should participate in whatsoever is done out of respect for the living; it should not participate in whatsoever is done out of respect for the dead.[1]

In the event that one has been declared an intentional suicide, Bahag, Alfasi, and Maimonides are in agreement that no funeral rites are performed; no mourning is observed, no lamentation is made, but the relatives stand in line (to be comforted); the mourner's benediction is recited, and all that is intended as a matter of honor for the living is done.[2]

Naḥmanides' position on the procedures of mourning for an intentional suicide differs from his predecessors'. His view is that members of the family must rend their clothes, since it is an obligation. This is indicated, in his view, by the textual requirement that the relatives stand in line and the mourner's benediction be recited.

The only situation, according to Naḥmanides, wherein no mourning is to be observed is when one is executed by the courts.[3]

R. Solomon b. Adret clarified that the statement "no rites

whatever should be observed" does not refer to burial and shrouds but (rather) that there should be no rending of clothes, baring of shoulders, or a eulogy.[4]

The Tur (Y.D. 345) follows the view of Naḥmanides with regard to the obligation of the immediate relatives to rend their clothes.

The *Shulḥan Arukh (Yoreh De'ah* 345) is in agreement with Maimonides that no rites of mourning whatever are to be observed for the deliberate suicide. However, all rites that honor the living are to be observed.

Tuktzinski indicates that in the case of an intentional suicide, the mourners do not observe the laws of an *onen*.[5] The procedure of *onen* is based on the obligation of the mourner to bury his deceased relative. This in turn is based on the positive commandment for the *kohen* to defile himself for an immediate relative.[6] The *kohen*, however, is not obligated to mourn for an intentional suicide.[7] The obligation, then, to bury the suicide is based on the verse "you shall bury him" (*kavor tikb'renu*).[8] This is not necessarily the exclusive obligation of the mourners. Therefore, when there are others who can care for the deceased, the mourner is not obligated to observe the laws of the *onen*, neither from the standpoint of honoring the deceased nor because of the obligation to bury the dead.

The intentional suicide was to be buried apart from the other deceased, a distance of more than eight cubits, based on the principle "the wicked should not be buried next to the righteous."[9] This became accepted practice. "This was the practice in the old cemetery in Berlin, where there was a separate place for those who committed suicide; however, because of the pronouncement of the government, this practice was nullified, and they were buried without any differentiation."[10]

In *She'elot Ut'shuvot Mima'amakim*, Ephraim Oschry indicates that burying the suicide in a special place was the custom in Lithuania and Germany.[11]

R. Samuel Mohilever of Bialystok and R. Sholom Schwadron did not permit the removal of the remains of a suicide from where he had previously been buried. They were of the opinion that moving the remains of the deceased from grave to grave would be a desecration of the dead, even in the case of an intentional suicide.[12]

R. Moses Schreiber shows concern for the welfare of the survivors of an intentional suicide. He suggests that they be permitted to mourn, even if all the laws of intentional suicide apply. In his view, the honor of a Jewish family supersedes other considerations.[13] R. Aaron Azriel strongly disagrees. He indicates that the Torah condemned individuals from prominent families when necessary. He cites Ishmael and Esau, and notes that they were not spared to preserve the honor of Abraham and Isaac. He goes on to state that the Torah specifically forbids the showing of partiality to the powerful.[14]

R. Azriel is concerned that R. Moses Schreiber's view might eliminate the law regarding intentional suicide. R. Schreiber disputes the practice of not reciting *Kaddish* for an intentional suicide. His suggestion in such a case is for the deceased's son to convene a minyan at his home so that other mourners will not be deprived of their prerogatives. However, if there is the slightest doubt as to whether he was a deliberate suicide, his sons should recite the *Kaddish* in the synagogue.[15]

R. Kluger stipulates that all other mourners take precedence over the survivors of the suicide.[16]

R. Azriel disallows the recital of *Kaddish* in the case of an intentional suicide.[17]

In his responsa with reference to the recital of *Yizkor* for a suspected suicide, R. Judah Aszod determined that it is permissible. He based his decision on the following points made by R. Moses Schreiber: (1) there is an operative presumption of innocence, i.e., perhaps a panic seized him, and (2) where there is no loss to the other mourners, the son of the suspected suicide can say *Kaddish* for him.[18]

R. Chaim Eliezer Shapiro was asked whether a headstone could be placed on the grave of an individual who had died ten years before by his own hand, during a period of incarceration. R. Shapiro determined that it should be, as this was considered one of the burial requirements, and according to R. Solomon b.

Adret the suicide is not to be deprived of any of these necessities.[19]

The sources cited above demonstrate the following:

The intentional suicide was not afforded the full rites of burial and mourning, as these rites are an honor bestowed on the deceased, and the intentional suicide is clearly not deserving of this honor.[20] Naḥmanides' view that members of the family must rend their clothes is based on his opinion that this is an *obligation* on the mourners and is not to be seen as honoring the intentional suicide. Tuktzinski's view that the mourners for an intentional suicide are free of the laws of *onen* is also based on the central premise that the intentional suicide is not deserving of the usual honor bestowed on the deceased. In addition, the obligation to bury him is not specifically that of the remaining relatives. In order to emphasize the disdain with which his act was viewed, the intentional suicide was not to be buried near the other deceased.

However, there are other implications with regard to the intentional suicide. What will the effect be on the reputation and welfare of the survivors? Will the suicide of a family member cast aspersion on all of them?

R. Moses Schreiber responds to this by indicating that the family should mourn even though their relative may have been an intentional suicide. He also stipulates that *Kaddish* should be recited. These opinions parallel his view that suicide is associated with irrational behavior and consequently is to be treated with great leniency.[21] Although vigorous exception is taken to this by some authorities, the views of R. Schreiber with regard to the mourning rites observed by the family and the recital of *Kaddish* have been recognized by others.[22]

Excursus II

Suicide in Ancient Greece and Rome

The first explicit mention of suicide in Greek literature is the case of Epikaste (Jocasta), the mother (and wife) of Oedipus of Thebes in the Nekyia the land of the dead.[1] In the literature of ancient Greece there are many records of suicide or threats of suicide following bereavement. In the *Iliad,* Andromache says to Hector, "If I lose thee it were better for me to go beneath the earth."[2]

Cases are also recorded of suicide to escape the shame of sexual dishonor.[3] Suicide for patriotic reasons is often commended.[4]

One of the most famous suicides in Greek literature is that of Ajax, who took his life because of shame. He is the subject of Sophocles' play by that name. Motives of shame and dishonor are mentioned as causes of suicide by the historians of the fifth century. Herodotus relates the legend of Niktonis, who committed suicide by leaping into a room full of ashes to escape punishment for her misdeeds.[5] Thucydides tells of the mutual suicide of the Corcyraeans, who "cheated the hangmen."[6]

In Xenophon we find suicide of the romantic type wherein a faithful servant seeks to share the fate of his respected superior.[7] Suicide as an act of atonement, when one considers oneself responsible for another's death, is found in Pausanias[8] and Herodotus.[9]

There are also instances of relationships of such intensity that when one of the parties died, the other sought to follow.[10]

A. W. Mair suggests that this kind of attitude is based on Greek religious thought, which incorporated the hope of reunion in the hereafter.[11] Plato refers to it in *Phaedo:* "Ere now for human love, for dead wife, for dead son, many a man has gone willingly to the House of Hades, drawn by the hope that in the world beyond they might see and be with those they loved."[12]

In Xenophon an incident of compulsory suicide is mentioned.[13] The ancient Greek states did not legislate against suicide as long as it did not pose a serious threat to the community. Athenian law did not consider suicide a penal offense. The treatment of suicide in Athens was on a religious basis rather than a legal one. According to a statement in the tenth-century Byzantine lexicographer Suidas, suicides and other victims of violent and untimely death were buried in a special place.[14]

The attitude toward suicide in the philosophic schools differed greatly. The teachings of the Pythagoreans condemned suicide. The Orphic or Pythagorean school held that the soul in the body in undergoing a penitential discipline for antenatal sin.[15] Therefore, suicide is deemed a rebellion by the person against the will of God, as the individual must wait until it is fitting for God to set him free. The indication from Plato in *Phaedo* and *Laws* is that he condemns suicide.[16] Aristotle treats suicide as an offense against the state.[17] The Epicureans (since they believed that death was nothingness) were opposed to suicide, as indicated in their works.[18] In general it is felt by scholars that the Cyrenaics were also opposed to suicide.[19]

The attitude of Stoic philosophy was favorable toward suicide. In Stoic thought, life and death were neither morally good nor evil. Consequently, the question of suicide was dependent on whether life or death was preferable in a given situation. Suicide, then, in Stoic thought might be required by a man's duty to his country or his friends or because of severe pain or incurable disease.[20] On occasion, according to the Stoic view, relatively minor discomfort might lead to suicide.[21]

The Cynics, too, viewed suicide affirmatively, as illustrated by Diogenes recommending to Antisthenes that he commit suicide.[22]

Suicides committed either to escape intolerable shame or

for great causes which demanded the supreme sacrifice were prevalent in the period of the Roman kings and that of the Roman Republic.[23] A suicide to escape terrible dishonor is personified in Roman literature by the story of Lucretia.[24] An example of self-sacrifice for country is that of Decius, who fell at the battle of Sentinum in 295 B.C.E.[25]

The Romans regarded suicide by hanging as a shameful death; penalties were accorded this type of suicide.[26]

Suicide appears to have been quite common under the Roman Empire, due primarily to the popularity of Stoicism among the educated upper class. Many of the writers of the Empire deal with incidents of suicide in their works. Pliny the Younger describes the illness of a prominent lawyer, Titus Aristo, in the following manner:

> He [Titus] requested us to consult his physicians about the issue of his illness with the intention of voluntarily departing from life if his illness were incurable, while on the other hand, if it were merely to be difficult and tedious he would bear up and bide his time; for so much he thought was due to the entreaties of his wife, the tears of his daughter, even to us his friends, that he should not by voluntary death abandon our hopes if only they were not in vain.

Pliny continues with a personal observation.

> Such conduct I consider eminently high and praiseworthy. For to rush to death under the influence of an impulse and an instinctive feeling is no more than what many have done; but to deliberately weigh the motives for and against, and then as reason advises, to accept or reject the policy of life or death, that is the conduct of a great soul.[27]

Pliny also relates the death by suicide of the poet Silius Italicus, also because of incurable illness.[28]

Much of the cultured world at the time of the Empire held a view which might be termed advanced Stoicism with its general permissibility of suicide. Seneca spoke of voluntary death vis-à-vis old age.

I will not relinquish old age if it leaves my better part intact. But if it begins to shake my mind, if it destroys my faculties one by one, if it leaves me not life but breath, I will depart from the putrid or tottering edifice. I will not escape by death from disease so long as it may be healed, and leaves my mind unimpaired. I will not raise my hand against myself on account of pain, for so to die is to be conquered. But if I know that I must suffer without hope of relief, I will depart, not through fear of the pain itself but because it prevents all for which I would live.[29]

Suicide as a means of forestalling judgment is often referred to in the literature of the Roman Empire.[30] Normally the goods of a condemned person were confiscated and he forfeited the rites of burial. The suicide, however, did not always forfeit the rites of burial, and his will and bequeathals remained valid.[31]

During the Empire, compulsory suicide as a means of execution was utilized, the most famous examples being those of Lucan (Tacitus, *Annals* XV, 70), Seneca (ibid., XV, 60–63), and Petronius (ibid., XVI, 18).

Two distinguished contemporary scholars of suicidology have summarized the attitute toward suicide in Greece and Rome in the following manner:

Most authorities seem agreed that suicide was not considered a sin in the Greek or Roman State; that it was referred to with a certain degree of admiration in ancient legends and in Homer; that it was opposed by Pythagoras and other early philosophers, that the later schools of Greek and Roman philosophy took a more lenient attitude.[32]

Excursus III

Attitudes Toward Suicide in Christianity

The New Testament does not directly condemn suicide.[1] During the early years of the Church, several motives for suicide were viewed favorably. Certain acts of martyrdom which were not considered inimical to Christian doctrine involved individuals taking their own lives.[2] The early ecclesiastical writers narrate many of these situations with some admiration. They also approve another motive for suicide—a woman's defense of her honor. St. Ambrose and St. John Chrysostom eulogize St. Pelagia—a young woman of fifteen who after capture by soldiers obtained permission to retire to her room to dress, subsequently ascended to the roof of the house, and perished by throwing herself down.[3]

A Christian lady of Antioch named Domina had two daughters who were famous for their beauty and piety. They were captured during the Diocletian persecution. Out of fear of the loss of their chastity, all three cast themselves into a river and drowned.[4]

The tyrant Maxentius had become infatuated with a Christian lady, the wife of the prefect of Rome. She was unable to repulse his advances. She asked permission to retire briefly to her chambers and, while there, stabbed herself.[5]

Jerome did not condemn the austerities which might weaken the constitution of the individual. He relates approvingly the life and death of a young nun named Belsilla, who, at twenty, retired to a convent and expired there—partially as a result of the intense penances she inflicted upon herself.[6]

St. Augustine was the first to denounce suicide as a crime under all circumstances. This was to serve as the basic position of the Catholic Church even to the present day. In *The City of God* he deliberates at great length whether suicide may be condoned in the case of a woman whose honor is in danger, or for that matter at any time. He concludes that it is never an appropriate act. As summarized by H. J. Rose,[7] his reasons are that suicide is an act which precludes the possibility of repentance,[8] that it is a form of homicide and therefore a violation of the sixth commandment.[9] It is not justified by any of the exceptions to that commandment, which have been divinely established,[10] and is aggravated by the fact that the person thus killed has done nothing worthy of death.[11] Hence, suicide to avoid violation is at best the commission of a greater sin to escape a lesser.[12] However, there were unquestionably in St. Augustine's time several persons who had taken their own lives and were recognized officially by the Church as martyrs. He seeks to reconcile this difficulty by suggesting that in these cases a special divine ordinance superseded the general law, which nevertheless is in full force for ordinary persons.[13]

Augustine's teaching on suicide became firmly established and was eventually reflected in Church law. The Council of Arles (452) denounced suicide as a diabolical inspiration. The Synod at Auxerre (578) decreed in its seventeenth canon that no offering should be received from one who had taken his own life. The Council of Braga (563) denied full funeral rites to suicide, and the *Capitula* of Theodore, archbishop of Canterbury, provided that mass was not to be said for suicides, only prayers and alms were to be offered (canon 63). Attempted suicide was punished by the Council of Toledo (693) with exclusion from church fellowship for two months. In 1284 the Synod of Nimes refused burial in consecrated ground to suicides.[14]

In his *Summa Theologica,* Thomas Aquinas formulated the attitude that the Catholic Church has held ever since. He considered suicide a mortal sin against God, who has given life, and against justice and charity. His reasons are as follows:

(1) the taking of one's own life is contrary to the inclination implanted by the Creator in every creature to love itself, to conserve itself in existence, and to resist forces that would destroy it. (2) suicide is an offense against society. Man naturally belongs to society, as a part to a whole, and in taking his own life he deprives the community of something rightfully belonging to it.[15] (3) life is a gift that God gives to a man to use and enjoy, but in due submission to the power of Him who has dominion over death and life. Therefore he who takes his own life sins against God, just as one who kills a servant does an injury to the master to whom the servant belongs. (*ST*2a2ae, 64.5)[16]

The Code of Canon Law, which is the basic law of the Church, has a number of articles on suicide and self-mutilation.[17]

Canon 985:5. These people are considered irregular because of crime; those who mutilated themselves or others, or who attempted to deprive themselves of life.

Canon 1240 P, sec. 3. These are to be deprived of Christian burial unless they have given some signs of repentance before death; those who kill themselves deliberately.

Canon 1241. Those who are deprived of Christian burial are not to be given a funeral mass nor an anniversary mass nor any public funeral service.

Canon 2339. Those who have presumed to command or to force Christian burial to be given to infidels, apostates from the faith or heretics, schismatics, or others whether excommunicated or interdicted, against the prescriptions of Canon 1240.

1. These people contract excommunication automatically, which excommunication is not reserved to anybody. However, those who freely grant Christian burial to the above incur interdict preventing them from entering church. This interdict is reserved to the Ordinary (the local bishop).

Canon 2350. Those who bring about their death with their own hands when death actually follows—these are to be deprived of ecclesiastical burial in accordance with Canon 1240, P.L., sec. 3.

If death does not follow, they are to be prevented from exercising legitimate ecclesiastical acts, and if they are clerics, they are to be suspended for a length of time—that is to be defined (determined) by the Ordinary and they are to be removed from any benefices or offices having to do with the care of souls whether in the internal or external forum.

However, Franco Ferracuti, in an article entitled "Suicide in a Catholic Country," states:

It should be noted that, although the basic principle on which the law of the Church is based never changed, the practical application of the law has been somewhat lessened following the progress of psychiatric studies which consider many, if not all, suicides mentally abnormal. For example, suicide while in a state of mental abnormality is not subject to the penalty of exclusion from religious rites, and such deaths are not officially considered as suicides. Furthermore, this exemption is based upon a judgment about the mental condition of the deceased made by the priest himself. No expert opinion is required and no medical certificate is necessary. The decision is left entirely to the priest, and in case of doubt, he may presume mental abnormality and give sacred burial, provided there has been no great scandal and publicity. In a symposium held in 1949 by the Roman journalists, it was advocated that a minimum of publicity be given to suicide cases, in order to allow sacred burials in as many cases as possible.[18]

The recent magisterial teaching of the Church states the contemporary Catholic view of suicide most clearly.

Vatican Council II: "Furthermore, whatever is opposed to life itself, such as any type of murder, genocide, abortion, euthanasia, or willful self-destruction, whatever violates the integrity of the human person, such as . . . all these things and others of their like are infamies indeed."[19]

As a contemporary Christian scholar has written:

The Augustinian-Thomist position remains that of orthodox Catholicism, and indeed that of Christianity in general. Suicide is condemned as a violation of the (sixth) commandment as contrary to nature, a usurpation of God's prerogative, and a social wrong. Exclusion of repentance is also a constantly given reason for Christian condemnation. Death, and its acceptance, play a special part in Christian thought both as "the wages of sin" and because of the opportunity it affords for a final display of confidence and courage. "The Christian accepts death," says the Anglican report of 1959 on suicide, "as that signal occasion when he is finally to prove the love and power of God in Christ. He sees death as the last and crucial occasion for the testing of his faith, where victory is to be won in Christ and his redemption fulfilled." Protestantism influenced in part by its rejection of the doctrine of purgatory, has been no less uncompromising in its condemnation of suicide than Catholicism. Roman Catholic canon law imposes penalties for suicide and its attempt. Ecclesiastical burial is denied to those who commit suicide *deliberato consilio*. Anglican canon law does not penalize suicide directly, but canon 68 excludes from Christian burial those guilty of "crime without repentance." In the past this has been interpreted to cover suicide.[20]

The preponderant Christian view, then, is that suicide is a mortal sin; as such, the person who has taken his life is to be denied certain rites of the Church. There has been, however, a recent moderation in that view based on psychiatric studies which consider many suicides mentally abnormal. As a result, many suicides are today granted sacred burial by the Christian Church.

Excursus IV

Suicide in Psychiatric Literature

Psychiatric literature has most often viewed suicide as a final pathological act induced by intrapsychic struggles within the personality of the individual. Dr. James M. A. Weiss, in an article entitled "The Suicidal Patient," states as follows: "It appears likely that some degree of personality disintegration is the most important single variable in the etiology of suicide. . . . the evidence indicates that suicidal behavior is most often a symptom or a terminating act of psychiatric disorder not a free moral choice."[1]

That this is the dominant psychiatric view is borne out further by similar contemporary statements.

Dr. Stanley Yolles, in a lecture entitled "The Tragedy of Suicide in the U.S.," indicates that one of the modern hypotheses of suicide prevention is that "suicidal patients are just as disinclined to be ill, as for instance tuberculosis patients; they are not free in making their decisions to die."[2]

Dr. George Murphy, in an editorial entitled "Suicide and the Right to Die," writes: "So called rational suicide is a rarity. The descriptive facts are that most persons who commit suicide are suffering from clinically recognizable psychiatric illnesses."[3]

In order to understand suicide, psychiatric thinkers have sought to discover the psychological dynamics of depression, which is its most frequent precursor.

Karl Abraham stressed the central role of ambivalence in the mental life of the depressed patient. The quantities of love and hate are almost equal. Patients who are depressed are incapable of love because they hate whenever they love. The sadism which the depressed person turns on himself stems

73

from the internalization of a sadism originally directed externally.[4] Abraham surmised that "depression results from an attitude of the libido in which hatred predominates."[5]

Sigmund Freud sought to further understand, in precise fashion, the dynamics of suicidal behavior. In his *Psychopathology of Everyday Life,* Freud speaks of the instinct of self-destruction, which he considered quite prevalent.

> There is no need to think self-destruction rare. For the trend to self-destruction is present to a certain degree in very many more human beings than those in whom it is carried out; self injuries are as a rule, a compromise between this instinct and the forces that are still working against it, and even where suicide actually results, the inclination to suicide will have been present for a long time before in lesser strength, or in the form of an unconscious and suppressed trend.[6]

In his *Mourning and Melancholia,* Freud attempted to understand the mechanics of the intrapsychic struggle which brings about suicide. It was his view that melancholy and subsequent suicide are often the result of aggression directed at least partially towards an introjected[7] love object with whom the individual had previously identified himself.[8]

In a further explanation, Freud indicates that in melancholia and suicide,

> We find that the excessively strong superego which has obtained a hold upon consciousness rages against the ego with merciless violence. . . . What is now holding sway in the superego is as it were a pure culture of the death instinct, and in fact, it often enough succeeds in driving the ego into death.[9]

In discussing a case of attempted suicide, Freud asserted the following:

> Probably no one finds the mental energy required to kill himself unless in the first place in doing so he is at the same time killing an object with whom he has identified himself, and in the second

place is turning against himself a death wish which had been directed against someone else.[10]

In *Beyond the Pleasure Principle*, Freud postulated the theory of the death instinct.[11] Suicide is the most extreme evidence of its active element.

Karl Menninger, who is considered to be one of the foremost expositors of Freud's views in the United States, further developed and enhanced this position.

In *Man Against Himself,* he posits three sources of suicide. They are the impulses derived from the primary aggressiveness crystallized as a wish to kill; the impulses derived from a modification of the primitive aggressiveness; the conscience, which is crystallized as the wish to be killed. In his view, some of the original primary self-directed aggressiveness, the wish to die, joins hands with the more sophisticated motives and adds to the total vectorial force which impels the precipitate self-destruction.[12]

Fenichel, in his *The Psychoanalytic Theory of Neurosis*, states:

> From the standpoint of the ego, suicide is, first of all, an expression of the fact that the terrible tension that the pressure of the superego induces has become unbearable. Frequently the passive thought of giving up any active fighting seems to express itself, the loss of self-esteem is so complete that any hope of regaining it is abandoned. . . . To have a desire to live evidently means to feel a certain self-esteem, to feel supported by a protective force of a superego. When this feeling vanishes, the original annihilation of the deserted hungry baby appears.[13]

The view of many leading psychiatric thinkers with regard to suicide can best be understood within the structure and context of their total approach rather than through their precise description of the intrapsychic processes leading to suicide.

Jung stresses the self as the deeper center that maintains the relationship between the individual and the world, and denies the monopolistic role of the ego. For life to be meaningful and significant there must be minimal contact between the ego and the self.

Danger can ensue because the self has both a bright and a dark side; the latter when it prevails may make death seem preferable to life.[14]

According to Jung, the person with suicidal tendencies yearns, very often unconsciously, for a spiritual rebirth. As Dr. Bruno Klopfer has indicated: "In suicide, death is seen as the death of the ego, which has lost contact with the self and must return to the womb of the magna mater[15] to reestablish contact and to be reborn."[16]

In the Adlerian view of psychoanalysis, the individual must be seen as part of his social context and as a unique whole striving for a success that he defines in his own subjective terms, all of which he may not be aware of.

The mentally healthy striving represents a contribution or an asset to the social group, whereas mental disorder is a disturbance or liability to the group. In Adler's view, *social interest* is the criterion for appraising mental health. Dr. H. L. Ansbacher has written that in the view of Adler, inadequate social interest is likely to arise in children with organ inferiorities, in those who have been treated with hostility or neglected, and in those who have been pampered. The individual in all three groups is likely to see himself at a special disadvantage, not welcomed by the world or not able to obtain the special consideration that he tacitly demands. He is thus likely to develop increased inferiority feelings. Suicide may ensue as a result of intense inferiority feelings and a decided lack of social interest. Suicide, according to Adler, is a means of inflicting pain on others and is a manifestation of extreme self-centeredness.[17]

The suicidal person, in Adler's view, is ambitious and vain. The contemplation of suicide gives him the feeling of mastery over life and death. Adler characterizes this feeling as "the supreme expression of the goal of superiority on the useless side of life."[18]

According to the view of Henry S. Sullivan, human relatedness is at the center of character and personality. The "self" develops out of the organized experience with important others in a person's life. Personifications are the symbolic extension of organized experience in relationships which lead to the expectation of specific kinds of interpersonal contacts. Personifications continually occur throughout life. Unresolved conflicts occurring at different times with regard to relationships may, in predisposed persons, bring about mental illness, as indicated on occasion by suicidal attempts.[19]

As Dr. Maurice Green has written with regard to the Sullivanian approach to suicide,

> Suicide belongs in the category of hostile types of integration with other individuals. . . . Additional factors important in suicide are anxiety, which is a result of inadequate personifications and which may produce anti anxiety systems that may hamper growth, and envy, which takes place when the person cannot feel a sense of his own worth.[20]

It is Karen Horney's view, in opposition to Freud, that man is not born with innate destructive tendencies. Neurotic development has its beginnings in the infant. If the mother is an anxious person, she often relates to the child in a neglectful way. His early upbringing will be one filled with anxiety and contradictory patterns of behavior. These elements often induce in the child a process termed by Horney "basic anxiety." This process is the result of the child's trying to fashion a consistent position for himself. As a result of the child's trying to adjust himself to his parents, he becomes "outer oriented" instead of "self oriented." These forms of outer-orientation eventually appear as behavior patterns of authoritarianism, self-abnegation, or resignation.

In one of the early phases of neurotic growth, if the child is successful in overcoming his feelings of anxiety, he begins to feel superior. Another phase of neurotic development takes place if contradictory demands are constantly made upon the child. The child may master the anxieties entailed in this by seeking to balance them. If he achieves this, he may further develop feelings of superiority.

The next phase takes place when the child crystallizes his feelings of superiority and invests them with all sorts of power. This is the final phase, the formation of the "idealized self." By the time anyone comes to this stage of development, he has drifted far away from the development of the self. This process, which has separated the real self from the idealized self, Horney termed the "alienation of the self."

Feelings of self-hatred appear in a person living on the basis of idealized self-glorifying operations because of (as Horney puts it) "the rage of the proud self for feeling humiliated and held down at every step by the actual self." In further explaining Horney's view of suicide, Dr. L. De Rosis states:

> If the intensity of the self hatred is great and the possibility of its discharge non-existent and if the person has an extensive alienation from his self, suicide can ensue sometimes by design sometimes by accident. It is most often the person who has adapted the aggressive (or authoritarian) orientation to life who takes the active step towards self-destruction, whereas self-abnegators die through neglect of the self in the search for others to fill self-esteem, and resigned persons often die by inaction or default.[21]

In psychiatric thought, suicide is inextricably bound up with mental disease. It is the act of an individual whose life has been intensely handicapped by conflict, emotional deprivation, and maladjustment. It is a symptom of underlying illness, whose effects are as devastating as any physical malady, and is deserving of the most serious attention and preventive techniques.[22]

The views of those cited make it very clear that the suicidal individual suffers from pathological behavior prior to taking his life. The act of suicide is the culmination of much inner conflict, isolation, inferiority feelings, and lack of social interest. Although each of those cited understands the problem of the suicidal individual from a different perspective, all point to the intense maladjustment in the suicidal individual.[23]

Appendix

1. For a suicide, no rites whatsoever should be observed. Rabbi Ishmael said: "He may be lamented: 'Alas, misguided fool! Alas, misguided fool!' "

Whereupon Rabbi Akiba said to him: "Leave him to his oblivion: Neither bless him nor curse him!"

There may be no rending of clothes, no baring of shoulders, and no eulogizing for him. But people should line up for him, and the mourners' blessing should be recited over him, out of respect for the living. The general rule is: The public should participate in whatsoever is done out of respect for the living; it should not participate in whatsoever is done out of respect for the dead.

Who is to be accounted a suicide?

Not one who climbs to the top of a tree or to the top of a roof and falls to his death. Rather it is one who says, "Behold, I am going to climb to the top of the tree," or "to the top of the roof, and then throw myself down to my death," and thereupon others see him climb to the top of the tree or to the top of the roof and fall to his death. Such a one is presumed to be a suicide, and for such a person no rites whatsoever should be observed.

If a person is found strangled hanging from a tree, or slain impaled upon a sword, he is presumed to have taken his own life unwittingly; to such a person no rites whatsoever may be denied.

It happened that the son of Gorgos ran away from school. His father threatened to box his ears. In terror of his father, the boy went off and cast himself into a cistern. The incident was brought before Rabbi Tarfon, who ruled: "No rites whatsover are to be denied him."

Another incident is that of a child from Bene Berak who broke a flask. His father threatened to box his ears. In terror of his father, the child went off and cast himself into a cistern. The matter was brought before Rabbi Akiba, who ruled: "No rites whatsoever are to be denied him."

As a result of this, the Sages said: "A man should not threaten his child. He should spank him at once, or else hold his peace and say nothing.[1]

2. The whole matter depends upon the assessment of the circumstances of the case, which should be carefully considered. In this situation, it has been confirmed that he slept in the house with the door locked and no person was in the house with him. [It is, therefore, evident] that he wounded himself. [Moreover,] how could others come without their presence being noted by the neighbors? [It should be noted] too that murderers, who normally attack unexpectedly, could easily have stabbed him with [their] swords and spears. They would not delay themselves by [first] tying or hanging him, as they would fear that this would precipitate his screams.[2]

3. [His declared intention of doing away with himself is not sufficient for him to be considered a suicide,] but this is also true: where there is a definite action, such as where we had seen him strangled and hanging from a tree in such a way that it surely appears that he hanged himself, and it happened that one was found hanged in a room, which was closed from within in such a way that it seems as though he had shut it himself; or that he fell on his own sword; it is presumed that he, through his actions, committed suicide. *But in any case it is not considered deliberate, as we assume that a bad mood struck and a stupor seized him,* and *he was fearful lest the Gentiles would despoil him,* as in the case of Saul; and similar reasons which affect and change one's outlook. [But it is not really suicide] until we hear from his own lips, in a sober frame of mind, that he has come to this situation through anger or [evil] impulse [as Maimonides was careful to note in the first chapter of his Laws of Mourning]. But, aside from this, we always accept it as fact that either he did not kill himself at all, or, if he did, it was not done deliberately.[3]

4. It is not considered suicide unless they warned him first and he accepted the warning, saying, "Knowing this I [will still] do it." But if they did not warn him first, he does not fall under the category of suicide.[4]

Moreover, since I see that if we should halakhically accept the argument of the *Zapikhit Bidvash,* the law of (illegal) suicide would disappear. Everyone who commits suicide does so deliberately and with clear thought, and prior warning is not relevant, since all suicides kill themselves secretly, where no one can prevent their evil acts.

And because of this, in my humble opinion, it seems that it is now imperative to establish halakhic parameters in favor of preserving life. We *should* let those [who consider committing suicide] feel guilty. We should not, moreover, favor them [by stating] that if they had not first been warned they will be treated [as regards burial, etc.] like those who died [naturally] in their beds.

See too *Erekh Lehem,* no. 345, where it is noted that the "justifiction" prayer (*Tzidduk Hadin*) is not said over [the suicide], so that others might not say that suicide is completely normal, possibly leading an embittered person to copy it.[5]

5. And concerning what is said (*Abodah Zarah* 18a), "It is better that the One who gave life [the Lord] should take it back, and one should not kill himself," here [in *Gittin*] they feared torture, as it says (*Ketubot* 33b), "If they had lashed Hananiah, Mishael and Azariah, they would have worshipped the [golden] image." Another answer: one must note that they were immorally torturing them, but *were not [threatening them]* with death.[6]

6. It would seem that even if he was captured by Gentiles, and was afraid that they would torture him until he worshipped foreign gods, still he should not kill himself, and should suffer the tortures according to his capacity. And he who comes to purify himself is helped from heaven.

However, if one is afraid that he will be tortured for the sake of other Jews, and, God forbid, some Jews will be lost (as some false monarchs do, when they torture an individual Jew with reference to the general populace [apparently to get information], and one will thereby cause the death of many), one is permitted to kill himself, and perhaps Saul, of blessed memory, intended this when he fell on his sword, as he felt that if he fell alive into their hands they would violate him and torture him. And probably the children of Israel would not be able to see and listen to the difficulties of the king, and they would not prevent themselves from avenging him, and saving him, and consequently thousands of Israel would fall.

And possibly [Saul's suicide] was due to the fact that a king, who is the anointed of God, must not allow himself to die at the hands of Gentiles where death by torture and humiliation would, in the beliefs of our religion, bring about a desecration of God's name.[7]

7. Rabbenu Tam states that when there is a fear that the Gentiles would try to force Jews to transgress through unbearable torture, it is a mitzvah to commit suicide, as in *Gittin* 57b, where [Jewish] children, taken away for immoral purposes, threw themselves into the sea.[8]

8. Everytime R. Hiyya b. Ashi recited the *Taḥanun* prayer, he used to say, "The Merciful, save us from the Tempter." One day his wife heard him. "Let me see," she thought, "it is so many years since he has separated himself from me, why then should he pray thus?" One day, while he was studying in his garden, she adorned herself and repeatedly walked up and down before him. "Who are you?" he asked. "I am Haruta [a famous courtesan] and I have returned today," she answered. He then looked closely at her. She said to him, "Bring me that pomegranate from the uppermost bough." He jumped up, went, and brought it to her. When he reentered the house, his wife was setting the fire in the oven, whereupon he got up and sat himself down in [the oven] (to kill himself—Rashi). "What is this?" she asked. He told her what had occurred. She then told him, "It was I," but he ignored her until she gave him proof of this. "Nevertheless," he said, "my intention was evil." [Because of this,] that righteous man fasted all his life until he died thereof.[9]

9. The upright shall behold his face [Psalm 11:7]. The Sages say that during a time of religious persecution a decree was issued for the hanging of Jose ben Joezer. Jakum of Ṣĕroroṭ, the nephew of Jose ben Joezer of Ṣeredah, rode by on a horse as Jose ben Joezer, bearing the beam for the gallows, was going forth to be hanged. Jakum said: "Look at the horse that my master gives me to ride, and look at the horse that thy Master gives thee to ride." Jose ben Joezer replied: "If so much is given to such as thee who provoke Him, how much more shall be given to those who obey His will!" Jakum asked: "Has any man been more obedient to the will of God than thou?" Jose ben Joezer replied: "If so much is done to those who are obedient to His will, how much more shall be done to those who provoke Him!" This answer went into Jakum like the venom of a snake. He went away and imposed upon himself the four death penalties of stoning, burning, beheading, and strangulation. How did he do it? He got a beam and drove it into the ground. To the beam, he firmly tied a rope. He placed sticks of wood in a row and built a wall of stones over them. Then he piled up fuel in front of the beam and put a sword, pointing upward, in the midst of the fuel. After lighting a fire under the sticks of wood beneath the stones, he hanged himself from the beam and thus strangled himself. The rope broke, and he fell into the fire, the sword met him, and the wall of stones tumbled upon him. The soul of Jakum departed, and because of his repentance he was received. Jose ben Joezer, in the drowse of death, spied Jakum's bier flying through space and said: "See ye, this man by a brief hour precedes me into the Garden of Eden."[10]

10. Since the case where one says, "I will climb to the roof and jump," etc., and later he was found [dead] in other circumstances has not been totally clarified in the Talmud and later halakhic works, as to whether it constituted suicide or not, we must say that he can't be judged halakhically as a suicide, especially if he later repented [his earlier statement].[11]

[Still] it appears, in my humble opinion, that where there is a doubt in a case concerning the dignity of the individual, the halakhah must be interpreted in a strict manner. Therefore, in a case of doubtful suicide [the relatives] must mourn (It seems to me in my humble opinion). And despite [the facts in] our case, since the text in *Semahot* indicates precisely *va'met* ["and he died"]—from which we can deduce the following: either that there was doubt as to whether it really was a suicide, or that he admitted his deed and repented—he should be mourned. If so, in a situation where two factors point [in his favor and against suicide], he surely must be mourned.[12]

It is clear that if he really repents, he is not [later, if found dead,] considered a suicide, *as no obstacle is to be put before repentance.* This is similar to a situation in which those who withdraw from the community are not dealt with [punitively] as was laid down in chapter 345. Repentance [on their part] is effective, as Maimonides notes at the end of the third chapter of the Laws of Repentance.[13]

11. However, one can support the contention that it was publicly known that he was the killer, the poor man feared they would mistreat him and order him to be tortured and [then] put to death. He therefore chose to die without being tortured.

Now, [concerning] Saul, the text notes that he feared the Amalekites' abuse. We derive from this [the principle] that he who kills himself out of fear of torture is not considered a suicide. In our case, therefore, it is reasonable to assume that [since] he killed himself to save himself from torture, his death does not fall into the halakhic definition of suicide.[14]

12. In the case of a [Jewish] person, imprisoned by Gentiles, who fears that he will be sentenced either to death or to a prison term in a place where conditions may be considered more cruel than death, and where he feels that it is permitted to kill himself like King Saul, who [likewise] feared maltreatment, [and] so killed himself; this is not classified as suicide. *The general rule is that one should not be blamed for what he did in "great pain"; perhaps he lost his senses and was in a state of shock, Heaven forbid; and therefore he should not be judged a villain because of this;* his sons must say *Kaddish* [for him].[15]

13. Concerning your query regarding one who is destitute and went before two people with the statement "I despise life" and [then] kills himself, are his relatives allowed to mourn him? Since Maimonides in [his] Laws of Mourning decided, as the baraita *Semaḥot* maintains, that he is not to be mourned, does he mean that they do not have to mourn, but if they want to take pity on him, to maintain the [family] honor, [may they]?

In essence, we should not, Heaven forbid, judge this man to be a villain. The Midrash on the verse "Surely the blood of your lives will I require" comments: I might say that this applies to a case similar to Saul ben Kish, so it therefore says *akh* ["surely"]—and Saul only feared that he would be molested. We should not say, moreover, that it applies only when they would inflict rank humiliations upon him, thereby mocking the Israelites and bringing about a desecration of the Lord's Name, and not to others who kill themselves due to their many woes, worries, tribulations, or abject poverty; this makes no sense.

The theme of suicide is the denigration of human dignity, despising that which is good and scorning the world, as a few philosophers do in defiance of the Almighty, who prides Himself on His world, and sees it as praiseworthy, saying, "Thus shall it be." These [philosophers], however, say, "Not so." Some [even] say, moreover, that is praise for the soul which is removed from the dejected body, which serves as its grave, and similar foolish wickedness and lies.

But if he is in such great distress that he feels unable to withstand the pressure, and even if it is to prevent himself from sin—as calamities, evils, and even poverty confuse one even in matters concerning the relations with his Creator—there is no doubt that his actions do not constitute a wrongdoing.[16]

14. I have seen the responsum of the Rosh (no. 345) copied in the *Besamin Rosh* where one living in poverty killed himself. The response was that this could not legally be considered suicide. See there.

This idea, in my opinion, should be discarded, and such should not be affirmed in Israel. Moreover, I refuse to believe that these statements emanated from the lips of the Rosh, as all rabbinic authorities have indicated the opposite view; that it is considered suicide. . . .

And regarding his statement that poverty confuses one vis-à-vis [his duties to] his Creator, etc. First, there is free will, and anyone who isn't compelled through actual torture should surely be able to preserve his life. . . .

Moreover, even if one is confused vis-à-vis [his duties to] his Creator, these are not circumstances which bring him to transgressing [prohibitions] for which he must sacrifice his life! Only idol worship, illicit sexual intercourse, or murder [are in that category]. And if so, for these other transgressions, according to many authorities, even if they compel him physically to do them, he is not permitted to take his own life; and even according to those who would allow it, it can only be done if he would certainly have transgressed had he not committed suicide. In this case, however, where there are great doubts [about this], and there are many poor people living in innocence [his act] falls into the category of suicide.[17]

15. And go forth and learn from R. Ḥaninah ben Teradion, in the first chapter of *Abodah Zarah*, that even when he suffered intensely to the point that death was preferable to life, nevertheless, the officer, who by removing the tufts of wool [from his heart] hastened his death, [merited life in the world-to-come]. But [R. Ḥaninah] himself did not open his mouth to allow the flames to enter it. He considered it better that the One who gave [life] should take it back, and that he was not [permitted to] take control over himself [to commit suicide]. In this the [author of the] work, *Besamin Rosh*, in no. 345, is guilty of deception, and it has been substantiated that even if he is in terrible suffering, he is to be considered a murderer who died due to his own wickedness.[18]

16. A man should not send to his neighbor a barrel of wine with oil floating on top. It once happened that a man sent his friend a barrel of wine with oil floating on top. He went and invited some guests to partake of it. When they came, and he discovered that it was only wine [and he could not feed them], he went and hanged himself.[19]

The guests may not give to the son or daughter of the host from what is set before them unless they have the host's permission to do so. It once happened that a man in a time of scarcity invited three guests to his house, and he only had three eggs to set before them. When the child of the host entered, one of the guests took his portion and gave it to him, the second guest did likewise, and so did the third. When the father of the child came and saw him stuffing one [egg] in his mouth and holding two in his hands, he knocked him to the ground, so that he died. When the child's mother saw this, she went up to the roof and threw herself down and died. He too went up to the roof and threw himself down and died.[20]

17. It once happened that a certain student [upon entering a privy] left his tefillin in a hole adjoining the public way, and a harlot passed by and took them, and she came to the Beth ha-Midrash and said, "See what so-and-so gave me for my hire," and when the student heard it, he went to the top of the roof and threw himself down and killed himself. Thereupon they ordained that a man should hold them [the tefillin] in his garment and in his hand and then go in.[21]

18. Since, if he had committed a transgression involving the penalty of death, he is not to be executed, as is indicated in the Talmud, *Erubin* 65a, the sale or purchase of an intoxicated person is valid. If he committed a transgression involving the penalty of death, he is to be executed. . . . And R. Ḥanina concluded, "This applies only to one who did not reach the stage of Lot's drunkenness, but one who did reach such a stage is exempt from all responsibilities." It is surely evident that similarly, or all the more so, we do not consider him a suicide even though, simply stated, his sin was surely enormous, and Heaven forbid [it should ever occur]. Yet he cannot be considered a suicide.[22]

19. One person habitually became intoxicated. One day, because of his drunkenness, he drank poison. After his intoxicated condition eased, he was told that he had imbibed poison. He pleaded that doctors be brought to him to cure him. . . .

Inquiries should be made of his acquaintances and those who visited him while he was intoxicated to ascertain if he usually reached the stage of Lot's intoxication. We can then relate that [to the present case and conclude] that now too he reached the stage of Lot's intoxication. He should not, therefore, be considered a suicide, since one should be judged according to how he usually acts; and if he usually does not reach the stage of Lot's intoxication, he is to be considered a suicide, and even *Kaddish* is not to be said for him.[23]

20. Since the aforementioned R. David was on occasion of lucid mind and on occasion of unsound mind, and the agents of the law and the scribes came to investigate the matter and they asked what had happened to him, and he indicated that he had fallen and had not thrown himself down, and he lived one day and confessed appropriately, and he related all his affairs as a lucid man would—it was decided that when he threw himself down he was of unsound mind and afterwards he became lucid, and it was decreed that he be mourned and to do all appropriate things that are done for all the departed of Israel, and to bury him in the cemetery in the appropriate row, as is the custom.[24]

21. The general rule of suicide is that we relate it to any condition whatever, such as fear, suffering, or taking leave of one's senses, or that he felt it meritorious to do so, in order that he not commit other transgressions, and so on. [This must be the case] as it is truly unlikely to suppose that one does such a heinous act with a clear mind. Go forth and learn from [King] Saul, the righteous man, who fell on his sword so that the Philistines would not be able to abuse him. [That] and similar acts are called "acting under compulsion"; all the more so a child who commits suicide is to be considered someone who is not rational.[25]

22. On the day that Rabbi died, a *bat kol* went forth and announced: "Whosoever was present at the death of Rabbi is destined to enjoy the life of the world-to-come." A certain washerman who used to come to him [Rabbi] every day did not come that particular day. As soon as he heard this he went up upon a roof, fell down to the ground, and died. A *bat kol* came forth and answered: "That washerman is also destined to enjoy the life of the world-to-come."[26]

23. His disciples called out: "Rabbi [R. Ḥaninah b. Teradion], what do you see?" He answered them: "The parchments are burning, but the letters are soaring on high." "Open, then, your mouth," they said, "so that the fire will enter you." He replied: "Let Him who gave me [life] take it away, but no one may injure oneself." The executioner then said to him, "Rabbi, if I ease the flame and take away the tufts of wool from over your heart, will you take me into the life to come?" "Yes," he replied. "Then swear unto me." He swore unto him. He then raised the flame and removed the tufts of wool from over his heart, and his soul quickly departed. The executioner then jumped and threw himself into the fire. A *bat kol* exclaimed: "R. Ḥaninah b. Teradion and the executioner have been assigned to the world-to-come." When Rabbi heard it he cried, and said: "One man may acquire eternal life in a single hour, another after many years."[27]

24. Our Rabbis have taught: When the First Temple was about to be destroyed, bands upon bands of young priests with the keys of the Temple in their hands assembled, mounted the roof of the Temple, and exclaimed: "Master of the Universe, as we did not have the merit to be faithful treasurers, these keys are handed back into Thy keeping." They then threw the keys up towards Heaven. And there emerged the figure of a hand which received the keys from them. Whereupon, they jumped and fell into the fire. It is in an allusion to them that the prophet Isaiah laments: "The burden concerning the Valley of Vision. What ails you now, that you have all gone up to the housetops, you that are full of uproar, a tumultuous city, a joyous town. Your slain are not slain with the sword, nor dead in battle." Of the Holy One, blessed be He, too, it is said, "shouting and crying at the mount."[28]

Notes

Introduction

1. P. Solomon, "The Burden of Responsibility in Suicide and Homicide," *Journal of the American Medical Association* 199 (January 1967): 321–24.

2. B. Nelson, "Suicide Prevention: NIHM Wants More Attention for 'Taboo' Subject," *Science* 161 (August 1968): 766–67.

See p. 111 for notes for Bibliographical Essay.

Chapter 1

1. *Baba Kamma* 91b.

2. Genesis 9:5 (Old JPS Version).

3. R. Eleazar lived in Palestine in the latter part of the first century of the common era.

4. *Genesis Rabbah* 34:13. See too M. Margulies, ed., *Midrash Ha-Gadol al Hamisha Humshei Torah, Sefer Bereshit* (Jerusalem: Mosad Harav Kook, 1947), Bereshit 9:5. The Pesikta derives the prohibition from the sixth commandment. See William Braude, trans. and ed., *Pesikta Rabbati* (New Haven: Yale University Press, 1968). See also S. Buber, *Midrash Tanhuma* (Jerusalem, 1964) p. 67 (Introduction).

5. King Saul took his own life. See 1 Samuel 31:1–7. Hananiah, Mishael, and Azariah refused to bow to the golden image that Nebuchadnezzar had erected. As a result, they were cast into a fiery furnace, from which they were subsequently rescued, through an act of Divine Providence. See Daniel 3 .

6. The Targumim are the Aramaic translations of the Bible. The texts of Targum Onkelos, Jonathan b. Uziel (so-called), Targum Yerushalmi, and Peshitta were utilized.

7. See Hebrew Publishing Co. translation by I. Leeser; New JPS Version (1962); Anchor Bible; King James Version; Septuagint Bible translated by C. Thomson.

8. Rashi to Genesis 9:5.

9. Solomon ben Abraham Parhon, *Mahberet ha-Arukh* (Pressburg, 1844) s.v. *haser* ("missing").

10. Commentary of R. Joseph Bekhor Shor (Jerusalem, 1956), Genesis 9:5. See *Eduyot* 6:1 and *Berakhot* 27a for mention of the culpability of animals. See also Noah Cohen, *Tzaar Ba'ale Ḥayim* (Washington: Catholic University Press, 1959), pp. 11–15.

11. R. Baḥya, *Commentary on the Torah,* ed. C. B. Chavel (Jerusalem: Mosad Harav Kook, 1966), p. 119.

12. Meir Loeb Malbim, *The Torah and the Mizvah* (Vilna, 1927), p. 110.

13. "Even concerning the one who kills himself, the Almighty demands his life's blood from him; and when, if not after his death?" Hezekiah ben Manoah, *Commentary of Ḥizkuni* in *Mikra'ot G'dolot* (New York: Shulsinger, 1950), Genesis 9:5.

14. J. Z. Mecklenburg, *Ha-K'tav V'ha'kabbalah* (Frankfurt a.M., 1880), p. 80. "[*Karet*] involves the separation and distancing of the soul from its exalted spiritual associations. But, with such a punishment, there is no complete destruction of the soul itself. Truly, regarding such a severe sin, when one commits willful suicide, his punishment is more severe than *karet*, as the soul itself proceeds to complete and uttermost eternal destruction. This is included, in my opinion, in the term *kol ḥayah* [every beast] which I wish to define as 'the complete soul.' "

15. It is interesting that E. Durkheim in *Suicide* (Glencoe, Ill., 1951), p. 155, indicates that "only towards 1870 do they [the Jews] begin to lose their ancient immunity [to suicide]." This is roughly contemporaneous with Mecklenburg's time.

16. Charles Chavel, ed. and trans., *Commentary of Nahmanides on Genesis* (New York: Shilo, 1971), Genesis 9:5.

17. *Commentary of Radak on Genesis* (Pressburg, 1842), Genesis 9:5.

18. Commentary of Ibn Ezra in *Mikra'ot G'dolot,* Genesis 9:5.

19. S. D. Luzzatto, *Commentary of Shadal* (Tel-Aviv, 1965).

20. Don Isaac Abrabanel, *Commentary on the Torah* (Jerusalem, 1964), Genesis 9:5; Commentary of Sforno in *Mikra'ot G'dolot,* Genesis 9:5; M. Alsekh, *Torat Moshe* (Amsterdam, 1777), Genesis 9:5; N. Z. J. Berlin, *Ha'amek Davar* (Jerusalem, 1970), Genesis 9:5.

21. The fact that the Targumim and some biblical commentators do not follow the traditional explanation and interpretation has, in my opinion, implictions which will be discussed later.

Chapter 2

1. G. Margoliouth, "Suicide (Jewish)," *Encyclopedia of Religion and Ethics* (1925), 12:37–38; Louis Rabinowitz, "Suicide," *Encyclopaedia Judaica* (1972), 15:489–90.

2. Judges 16:28, 30.

3. *Genesis Rabbah* 66:3.

4. *Sotah* 10a. See also Rashi to Judges 16:26.

5. Targum Jonathan, Judges 16:28.

6. Judges 16:31.

7. Judges 16:28, 29, 31.

8. Samson's situation might serve as a precedent for one participating in an act of war, wherein he will, in all likelihood, lose his life.

9. This view differs with those scholars who have listed him as a suicide. See above, n. 1.

10. 1 Samuel 31:1–7.

11. That Saul's fears of Philistine brutality were justified is evidenced by their desecration of his remains. See 1 Samuel 31:8–11.

12. 1 Samuel 31:4–5.

13. 2 Samuel 1:6–10.

14. 1 Chronicles 10:1–6.

15. *Pirkei de-Rabbi Eliezer* (New York, 1946), chap. 33, a work of the eighth century C.E.

16. *Leviticus Rabbah* 26:7. Composed in the mid-seventh century C.E. See Zunz and Albeck, *Ha-Derashot B'Yisrael* (Jerusalem, 1947), pp. 80, 136.

17. Saadia (ben Joseph) Gaon, *Commentary of R. Saadia Gaon on the Torah,* ed. Y. Kapah (Jerusalem, 1963), Genesis 9:5. See too Saadia (ben Joseph) Gaon, *Emunot V'Deot,* ed. Y. Kapah (Jerusalem, 1976), sec. 10:8, 11.

18. *Genesis Rabbah* 34:13.

19. Kimhi on 1 Samuel 31:5.

20. Ibid.

21. Don Isaac Abrabanel, *Commentary on I Samuel* (Jerusalem, 1955), chap. 31.

22. In a similar vein he cites the statement of Agag, king of Amalek: "The bitterness of death has vanished" (1 Samuel 15:32).

23. 2 Samuel 17:23.

24. *Makkoth* 11a.

25. Ibid.

26. Kimhi on 2 Samuel 17:23.

27. Meir Loeb Malbim, *Malbim on II Samuel* (Wilno, 1911), 17:23.

28. *Sanhedrin* 10:2. This mishnah includes Ahithophel with Balaam, Doeg, and Gehazi. Ahithophel is also thus characterized in *Aboth de-Rabbi Nathan,* chaps. 36 and 41. See also R. Israel Lifschitz's discussion of Ahithophel. *Mishnah Tifereth Israel* (New York, 1969), *Sanhedrin* 10:2. *Sanhedrin* 104b and 105a and *Numbers Rabbah* 14:1 indicate, however, that Ahithophel does have a share in the world-to-come.

29. 1 Kings 16:18.

30. Ibid., Kimhi.

31. 2 Maccabees 14:41–42. A suicide by a non-Jew, Ptolemy, who supported the Judeans at the Syrian court, is mentioned in 2 Maccabees 10:13.

32. See Excursus II, "Suicide in Ancient Greece and Rome," especially the discussion on Stoicism.

33. This is also true of Ahithophel.

Chapter 3

1. The texts utilized are M. Higger, ed., *Semaḥot*, (New York, 1931), and Dov Zlotnick, ed. and trans., *Tractate "Mourning" (Semaḥot)*, Yale Judaica Series, XVII (New Haven: Yale University Press, 1966). In the third chapter of his introduction, Higger says that the laws of suicide are found only in *Semaḥot* and nowhere else in talmudic literature. Zlotnick, in his introduction, pp. 1–9, concludes that *Semaḥot* is of the tannaitic period.

2. *Semaḥot* 2:1 (Zlotnick Trans.).

3. Ibid. The word in the MS Oxford Opp. 276 (Neubauer 370:6) which served as the basis of Zlotnick's translation is *nishla*, i.e., "fool." However, in other MSS the word reads *natla*, i.e., "one who has taken his own life." See also *Semaḥot* 2:1, Zhitomir and the *Biur Hagra* and *Nahlat Yaakov* commentaries.

4. *Semaḥot* 2:1 (Zlotnick Trans.).

5. Ibid. There may be no rending of clothes. The understanding of the provision is a subject of debate among the authorities. Maimonides, *Yad (Ebel* 1:11) states that no one is obligated to rend his clothes for the intentional suicide. Naḥmanides' position is that members of the family must rend their clothes, since it is an obligation. See Naḥmanides, *Torat ha-Adam, Kitvei Ramban, II*, ed. C. B. Chavel (Jerusalem: Mosad Harav Kook, 1964), p. 83

6. *Semaḥot* 2:1 (Zlotnick Trans.).

7. Ibid.

8. As there is no proof of intent.

9. *Semaḥot* 2:2 (Zlotnick Trans.). See also Excursus II, "Suicide in Ancient Greece and Rome." Compare incidents in Greek society in which there were clear statements of suicidal intent followed by the suicidal act.

10. Ibid.

11. Ibid., 2:3.

12. Gorgos is the name mentioned in the baraita. His identity is unknown.

13. *Semaḥot* 2:4 (Zlotnick Trans.).

14. Ibid., 2:5. See Sec. 1 of the Appendix for the text of *Semaḥot* 2:1–5.

15. Naḥmanides, *op. cit.*, p. 84.

16. *Baba Kamma* 8:4.

17. *Semaḥot* 2:4 (Zlotnick Trans.).

18. Rabbenu Asher, *Mo'ed Katan*, chap. 3, no. 94.

19. *Yoma* 82a. See also E. Z. Margolioth, *Bet Ephraim, Yoreh De'ah, Hilkhot Avel* (New Israeli ed., 1968), question 76.

Chapter 4

1. *Semaḥot* 2:2 (Zlotnick Trans.).

2. The emphasis as indicated throughout this chapter is my own.

3. See *Baba Mezia* 21b for similar usage of the term *da'at* to indicate deliberate intention. See Rashi's interpretation: *aveidah mida'at hi* (the owner) is aware of his loss.

4. The Rome MS of the *Halakhot G'dolot* (Berlin, 1888). See J. Hildesheimer, ed., *Halakhot G'dolot* (Jerusalem, 1972), *Hilkhot Avel*, p. 445. This edition is based on the MS Ambrosiana in Milan. This text, however, is not found in the Warsaw 1875 ed. of *Halakhot G'dolot*.

5. See *Kiddushin* 6b, *Gittin* 74a, *Sukkah* 41b.

6. Alfasi, *Mo'ed Katan* 1254.

7. *Yad, Ebel* 1:11.

8. *Yad, Gerushin* 2:13. See Tosefta *Gittin* 6:9, P. T. *Gittin* 6:8, and R. Abraham b. David on *Yad, Gerushin* 2:13, for further emphasis on the principle of immediacy.

9. *Haggahot Maimuniyyot, Yad ha-Ḥazakah, Gerushin* 2:13.

10. Margolioth, *op. cit.*

11. Margolioth, ibid., understands the phrase *shehayah meizar* ("he was afraid") to mean that his ascent was difficult, not that his mood at the time of his ascent was one of fear. In his view, if his mood was one of fear, the individual would be inculpable.

12. Chavel has emended the text to read: " 'See, I am climbing the tree,' and he fell [*v'nafal*] and he died." However, the use of the verb *nafal* ("fell") instead of *nofel* ("falls") would change the statement entirely. Chavel's emended statement, *v'nafal umet* ("and he fell and died"), does not have the same connotation of intent as *v'nofel umet* ("and he falls and dies"). See Naḥmanides, *op. cit.*, pp. 83–84.

13. R. Asher, *Mo'ed Katan*, chap. 3, no. 94.

14. Later authorities termed this a *ḥezkat kashrut* (presumption of innocence). See J. M. Tuktzinski, *Gesher ha-Ḥayyim* (Jerusalem, 1960), pt. I, chap. 25, sec. 1–3, for an interesting contemporary explanation which enhances the presumption of innocence.

15. *Semaḥot* 2:3.

16. *Halakhot G'dolot*, ed. Hildesheimer, p. 445; Naḥmanides, op. cit., p. 84; R. Asher, *Mo'ed Katan* 3:94.

17. *Yad, Ebel* 1:11.

18. Judah Ayash, *Shevet Yehudah* (Leghorn, 1783), *Yoreh De'ah*, chapt. 345. See Appendix, sec. 2. There is a paucity of responsa with regard to suicide until the nineteenth century. In all probability this is indicative of the infrequency of its occurrence until that time.

19. M. Sofer, *Responsa of the Ḥatam Sofer* (Vienna, 1895), *Yoreh De'ah*, responsum 326. See Appendix, sec. 3.

20. H. Pontremoli, *Zapikit B'dvash* (Salonika, 1848), chap. 67. See Appendix, sec. 4.

21. *P'at ha-Sadeh,* Appendix to *S'deh Hemed* (New York, 1962), s.v. *aveilut,* note 17.

22. *Semahot* 2:1.

23. Above, p. 13.

24. Emile Durkheim, *Suicide* (Glencoe, Ill.: Free Press, 1951), p. 155.

25. Nahmanides, *op. cit.,* p. 84; R. Asher, *Mo'ed Katan.*

26. A. I. Kook, *Mishpat Kohen* (Jerusalem, 1937), no. 144.

27. "And Saul said to his armor-bearer, 'Draw your sword and run me through with it, lest these uncircumcised men come and run me through and mock me' " (1 Samuel 31:4). See Appendix, sec. 5, for text of Tosafot.

28. R. Meir ben Barukh of Rothenburg, *T'shuvot, P'sakim U'Minhagim,* collected by I. Z. Cahana (Jerusalem, 1962), II, chap. 59.

29. For a contemporary discussion as to whether one is obligated to save an individual who has placed himself in danger, see Y. Gershuni, "Hayalei Yisrael hamistaknim neged p'kudah shel hakazin im yesh mizvah l'hazilan," *Or Hamizrach* 21 (1972): 3–8.

30. S. Luria, *Yam Shel Shlomo* (Prague, 1715), *Baba Kamma* chap. 8, no. 59. See Appendix, sec. 6.

31. Y. Gershuni, "M'ragel l'tovat hazibur she'nitpas im rasha'i l'abed azmo lada'at," *Or Hamizrach,* 21 (1972): 218–22.

32. In *Rabboteinu Ba'alei ha-Tosafot al Hamisha Humshei ha-Torah* (Jerusalem, 1967), Genesis 9:5, there is a singular opinion which condemns Saul for taking his own life. It views his suicide as occurring *shelo b'da'at hakhamim* ("without the consent of the Sages"). My suggestion as to the reason for this view is that the presumption of innocence is *not* assumed in Saul's case, since *there was no certainty* that his capture would lead to torture and humiliation. In all probability, the view here is that he should have fought unto death rather than take his own life. This opinion, however, is discounted by virtually all other authorities.

33. Tosafot *Avodah Zarah* 18a, s.v. *v'al.* See Appendix, sec. 7, for the text of this Tosafot. See, however, the view of the Ritva, cited by Luria, which indicates that it is permissible, rather than obligatory, according to R. Tam.

Chapter 5

1. Stoning, burning, decapitation, and strangulation.

2. L. Finkelstein, *The Pharisees* (Philadelphia: Jewish Publication Society, 1940), p. 594, associates Jakum with Alcimus, the high priest mentioned in 1 Maccabees 7:12. In his view, Jose b. Joezer was among the sixty Hasidim killed by Alcimus. This assumption, however, is unlikely. Jose b. Joezer is not

mentioned at all in 1 Maccabees. Alcimus is described in 1 Maccabees as dying from a sudden stroke and not through a suicide. In the Midrash, Jakum obviously died before R. Jose. In 1 Maccabees, the Hasidim were killed a year before Alcimus' death. Hence Jakum and Alcimus could not be the same person. I am grateful to Dr. Leo Landman, professor of Jewish history at Yeshiva University, for bringing this to my attention.

3. *Berakhot* 3a, 8b; *Shabbath* 32a; *Pesahim* 112a; *Taanit* 5b; *Baba Kamma* 61a; *Yoreh D'e'ah* 116. See Appendix, secs. 8 and 9, for the situations of R. Hiyya b. Ashi and Jakum of Zeroroth.

4. J. Reischer, *Shevut Ya'akov* (Prague, 1629), II. *Yoreh De'ah* responsum 111.

5. Ibid.

6. H. J. Azulai, *Birkei Yoseph* (Leghorn, 1774), *Yoreh De'ah* no. 345, in the name of the *Y'fei Tohar* on *Genesis Rabbah,* chap. 65. I have not found this view in the available texts. Yet, see *Y'fei To'har* on *Genesis Rabbah* 34:13. There, the author comments that the word *akh* ("and surely") in Genesis 9:5 ("and surely the blood of your lives will I require") excludes a case like that of Saul, since he surely knew that he would die, as he had already been informed. "Tomorrow you and your sons will be with Me" (1 Samuel 28:19). But, for another person, if he is surrounded by enemies, and a sharp sword lies upon his neck, he is not allowed to take his own life in anger or despair of [the Lord's] compassion, as the Lord in His Mercy will save even those taken to die and those who feel death approaching."

7. S. Kluger, *Responsa ha-Elef L'kha Shlomo* (Jerusalem, 1967), *Yoreh De'ah* no. 301; M. Schick, *Responsa of Maharam Schick* (Munkács, 1882), *Yoreh De'ah,* no. 346; R. Kobo, *Responsa Sha'ar Asher* (Salonika, 1877), *Yoreh De'ah,* no. 67. See Appendix, sec. 10.

8. H. Azulai, *Hayyim Sha'al* (Leghorn, 1792), no. 41. See Appendix, sec. 11.

9. S. Luria, *Yam Shel Shlomo* on *Baba Kamma* (Prague, 1715), chap. 8, no. 59.

10. "Derekh klal ein adam nitpas al za'aro." M. Banet, *Parashat Mordecai* (Signet, 1889), *Yoreh De'ah,* nos. 25–26. See Appendix, sec. 12.

11. S. Berlin, *Responsa Besamim Rosh* (Berlin, 1793), no. 345. See Appendix, sec. 13.

12. R. Saul Berlin, who issued the *Besamim Rosh,* claimed that it was a collection of responsa by R. Asher b. Yehiel. He indicated that he had only supplemented the work with his own notes. Because of the many controversial opinions in that work, it was felt by many of Berlin's contemporaries that the claim of R. Asher b. Yehiel's authorship was fraudulent and that Berlin actually wrote the work himself. Among those who opposed the work were R. Solomon Kluger and R. Mordecai Banet.

13. S. Kluger, *Responsa Tuv Ta'am Va'Da'at,* 3rd ed. (New York, n.d.), Laws of Mourning, no. 202. See Appendix, sec. 14.

14. M. Sofer, *Responsa Hatam Sofer* (Pressburg, 1858), *Even ha-Ezer*, no. 69.

15. See above "There is no doubt that there is nothing here which is prohibited at all." It should be pointed out, however, that E. Z. Margolioth and Sholem Schwadron accept Berlin's view.

16. "And concerning his question about that which occurred in your jurisdiction where several upstanding men, in order to free themselves from anguish, torment, misfortune, and embarrassment, committed suicide, Heaven forbid. Do we judge them in all respects as if they died in their beds [naturally], and do not deny them anything [proper funeral rites . . . or not]? Such a person is not to be judged halakhically a suicide, and nothing should be denied him." S. Schwadron, *Responsa of Maharsham* (Jerusalem, 1968), *Yoreh De'ah*, no. 123.

17. J. M. Tuktzinski, *Gesher ha-Ḥayyim* (Jerusalem, 1960), I. chap. 25, nos. 1–3.

18. I.e., whether the deceased should be eulogized, and the like.

19. This incident is related in essentially the same fashion in *Derekh Eretz Rabbah*, chap. 9. See Appendix, secs. 16 and 17, for the incidents cited in *Ḥullin* 94a and *Berakhot* 23 a (see below).

20. Above, p. 31. See also Abrabanel's understanding of Saul's suicide in light of this view, *above*, p. 31.

21. Y. M. Ginsburg, *Mishpatim L'Yisrael* (Jerusalem, 1956), pp. 257–262, wherein he discusses the matter of dueling and the penalties associated with it.

22. H. H. Medini, *S'deh Hemed* (Warsaw, 1891), *Aveilut*, no. 121. See Appendix, sec. 18.

23. A. Azriel, *Kapei Aharon* (Jerusalem, 1898), sec. 2, *Hilkhot Aveilut*, no. 16. See Appendix, sec. 19. It is of interest that chronic alcoholism is often associated with "successful" suicide attempts. See James M. A. Weiss, *The Suicidal Patient*, ed. Silvano Arieti, vol. 2 (New York: Basic Books, 1966), pp. 122, 125–26.

24. Y. Lampronti, *Paḥad Yizhak* (Venice, 1831), letter *mem*, no. 1. See too H. Azulai, *Birkei Yosef* (Leghorn, 1774), chap. 345, no. 72.

25. J. M. Epstein, *Arukh ha-Shulḥan* (New York, 1961), *Yoreh De'ah* chap. 345, no. 5. See Appendix, sec. 21. H. Posek, *Hillel Omer* (Tel-Aviv, 1956), *Yoreh De'ah*, no. 211.

26. George Murphy, "Suicide and the Right to Die," *American Journal of Psychiatry* 130 (April 1973): 472. See Excursus IV, "Suicide in Psychiatric Literature," for the psychiatric view of suicide.

27. R. Judah Hanasi.

28. *Kethubot* 103b. See Appendix, sec. 22.

29. See J. Greenwald, *Kol Bo al Avelut* (New York: 1956), p. 318, where this view is alluded to.

30. In P. T. *Ketubot* 12:3 there is also a discussion of this incident. Along with the description of this event, there is a passage which describes the prolongation of the eve of the Sabbath at the time of Rabbi's death, which took place on a Friday, so that no one involved in paying homage to his memory would be guilty of desecrating the Sabbath. A commentator has understood the launderer's suicide as taking place because he desecrated the Sabbath. *Korban ha-Edah*, T. J., *Ketubot* 12:3. s.v., *keivan*. In my opinion, this is not the case. There is no mention at all of the Sabbath in the description of the incident in the Babylonian Talmud. In the description found in the Palestinian Talmud, it is clear that the launderer took his life due to the remorse he felt at forfeiting a share in the world-to-come.

31. See Appendix, sec. 23, for description of R. Ḥaninah's predicament. There are some ancillary aspects to this situation. It appears that some of the Sages of Israel were viewed as having the ability to grant others (even non-Jews) a share in the world-to-come. It is also noteworthy that Rabbi's name is here, too, associated with a suicide. This, however, may be only a coincidence. The case of the Gentile executioner demonstrates that the righteous Gentile has a share in the world-to-come. Rabbi obviously approved of what he did.

32. Psalms, 113:9.

33. I am unaware of this tradition.

34. *Ta'anit* 29a. See Appendix, sec. 24.

35. Ibid.

36. Isaiah 22:1–2.

Chapter 6

1. See above, pp. 29–31.

2. Isaac of Corbeil, *Amudei ha-Golah* (reprinted in Israel, 1968), precept no. 3.

3. Meir ben Barukh of Rothenburg, *T'shuvot, P'sakim U'Minhagim*, collected by I. Z. Cahana (Jerusalem, 1962), II, no. 59. "Surely, one who martyrs himself for the declaration of the unity of God is permitted to commit suicide."

4. A. I. Kook, *Mishpat Kohen* (Jerusalem, 1937), no. 144. Rabbi Kook understands this from Asheri, *Mo'ed Katan*, chap. 3, par. 94. "And, similarly, we find in the case of an important man who committed suicide because he was being abused and debased like Saul, king of Israel, whose suicide was deemed permissible to him."

5. Naḥmanides, op. cit.; S. Luria, *Yam Shel Shlomo, Baba Kamma*, chap. 8, no. 59.

6. Josephus, *Jewish War*, VII, 8–9. For Josephus' views on suicide and procedures related to it, see ibid., III, 8, 361–92.

7. In recent years a substantial controversy has arisen with reference to Masada, and many studies and articles have been written about it. Among the recent articles that deal with Masada are the following: T. W. Rosmarin, "Masada, Josephus and Yadin," *Jewish Spectator*, October 1967; idem, "Masada Revisited," ibid., December 1969; B. Heller, "Masada and the Talmud," *Tradition* 10, no. 2 (1968): 31–37; S. B. Hoenig, "The Sicarii in Masada— Glory or Infamy?" ibid., 12, no. 1 (1970): 5–30; S. Spero, "In Defense of the Defenders of Masada," ibid., 12, no. 1 (1970): 31–43.; L. I. Rabinowitz, "The Masada Martyrs According to the Halakhah," ibid., 12, no. 3 (1970): 31–37; Z. Kolitz, "Masada—Suicide or Murder?" ibid., 12, no. 1 (1971): 5–26; D. I. Frimer, "Masada in the Light of Halakhah," ibid. 12, no. 1 (1971): 27–43; S. B. Hoenig, "Historic Masada and the Halakha Tradition," ibid. 13, no. 2 (1972): 100–115; R. Alter, "The Masada Complex," *Commentary* 56, no. 1 (1973).

I am grateful to Dr. L. D. Hankoff, professor of psychiatry at New York Medical College, for sending me his study, "The Concept of Suicide in the Life and Works of Flavius Josephus" (see Bibliography).

It would seem that Naḥmanides' interpretation of King Saul's act (that it was done because of intolerable stress) would be analogous to the situation at Masada, and suicide under such circumstances would be a permitted act. It would also be fitting, in my opinion, to compare the situation at Masada with that described in *Gittin* 57b. The Gemara indicates that four hundred youngsters were taken to Rome for shameful purposes. The Romans, then, took captives and used them for their immoral purposes. The defenders of Masada certainly feared a potentially similar fate. This would make suicide at least a permissible act; according to R. Tam, possibly an obligatory one. The opinion of such rabbinic luminaries as Naḥmanides, Asheri, *Tur Yoreh De'ah*, *Shulḥan Aruch Yoreh De'ah*, and R. Tam would seem to actually support such conduct rather than decry it. In this writer's view, whatever the merits of the other arguments relating to Masada, the defenders cannot be condemned on account of their mass suicide.

8. See H. Taubes, *Ozar ha-Ge'onim on Sanhedrin* (Jerusalem, 1967), p. 428. A geonic opinion is cited therein which indicates that *yehareg* includes suicide. See also *Bedek ha-Bayit on Bet Yosef, Tur Yoreh De'ah*, no. 157 for his discussion on this matter. He discusses both possibilities, i.e., whether *yehareg v'al ya'avor* includes suicide or not, but does not come to any conclusions. See *Ḥiddushei R. Yonah* (Jerusalem, 1968), *Sanhedrin*, end of chap. 8. He indicates that *yehareg v'al ya'avor* does not include suicide.

9. The Hebrew words are *bein shein* ("between the teeth"), of which *bashan* is considered to be a contraction. Talmudic translations are from the Soncino edition, London, 1936.

10. See Abraham Ibn Daud, *Sefer Ha-Qabbalah*, ed. Gerson Cohen (Philadelphia, 1967), pp. 63–64, for his account of an episode of suicide as an act of

martyrdom similar to that found in *Gittin* 57b. His account is laudatory and affirmative. See also *Lamentations Rabbah* 1:45.

11. A. M. Habermann, *Gezerot Ashkenaz v'Zarfat* (Jerusalem, 1946), p. 19. "And at that time honorable women went, hand in hand, saying, 'Let us go to the river and drown ourselves, so that the Lord's Name not be blasphemed because of us; as that which was holy has become like that which is trampled in the streets, with our precious ones becoming fuel for the flames, and death is preferable to us than life' " (anonymous author).

12. Each of the above incidents is considered a *kiddush hashem* of the highest order. In Speyer: "There was an important and pious woman there who martyred herself; she was the first of those martyred, either by execution or suicide, in all [our] communities."

In Worms: "And among those who were martyred, fulfilling [the verse] 'The mother was dashed to pieces with the children' (Hosea 10:14), mothers did fall on their children as they were [actually] slaughtered upon them." Ibid., p. 25.

In Mainz: "Then they all cried out in a loud voice, saying as one, 'We cannot wait any longer, as the enemy is already upon us. Let us quickly go and offer ourselves as a sacrifice before the Lord. And whosoever has a [slaughtering] knife should inspect it lest it have a defect; [then] let him come and slaughter us to sanctify the Eternal Life. He should then slay himself by slashing his throat or by sticking the knife in his stomach.' " Ibid., p. 31.

In Xanten: "Now let us rise and go to the Lord's House and quickly do the will of our Creator, as the enemy is upon us today, to slaughter on the Sabbath, each man and his son, his daughter, and his brother . . . and no man should take pity on himself or on his friend. The last survivor should commit suicide, using his knife to slash his throat or his sword to pierce his stomach, so that the impure ones shall not defile us . . . and we should offer ourselves as a sacrifice to the Lord, like a burnt offering to the Most High." Ibid., p. 48.

R. Solomon b. Samson was a scholar who lived in Worms in the eleventh century. He was a contemporary of Rashi.

13. R. Joseph ha-Kohen ha-Rofeh, *Emek ha-Bakha* (Jerusalem, 1956), p. 21. "And a Jewess by the name of Gutalda was apprehended in Ispork and, refusing to have her honor violated, sanctified God's name by drowning herself in the river. May the Lord remember her for good and avenge her!"

14. Ibid., p. 31. "And it came to pass in the year 1191 . . . that the [Christians] attacked God's nation in the city of York, England, on Shabbat ha-Gadol, filling them with great anxiety; whereupon they fled into their synagogue. The rabbi, Rabbi Yom Tov, arose and martyred some of those assembled there, and others too took weapons [to do likewise] on that day of violence. There was one who ordered his only son, who had not yet 'ventured to set his feet upon the ground,' to be slaughtered; and there were those who were burnt to death, thereby sanctifying Israel's God."

15. Habermann, *Gezerot Ashkenaz v'Zarfat*, p. 168.

16. Ibid., p. 171. The author's name is Solomon ben Abraham. Habermann says about him that "it seems he is the same R. Solomon ben R. Abraham who was in correspondence with R. Baruch ben R. Samuel of Mainz."

17. Named for the nobleman who led the persecutions.

18. Habermann, *Gezerot Ashkenaz v' Zarfat*, pp. 223–25.

19. Joseph ha-Kohen, *Emek ha-Bakha*, p. 41. "And the news reached in the environs of Bordeaux and Castile, Carcassonne and Agen that they intended to destroy all the Jews found there. In the regions of Toulouse, Burgundy, Marseilles, Conteau, and in many other cities, one hundred and ten communities were [destroyed] by the Shepherds' Edict. And many chose to kill their brothers and friends before the enemy approached, as the hidden Jews of Castile and Carcassonne did when they cast lots to see who would be the ones to kill their brothers. They all died then, with the last two survivors jumping from the tower to their deaths."

20. *Emek ha-Bakha*, pp. 46–47. "Many Jews gathered in their houses and locked themselves in when they saw that danger was approaching and fired their houses. And the fire consumed their houses, and those of their neighbors were set ablaze. And in the city of Mainz, the large bell in the belfry was [actually] split asunder because of the all-consuming fire. Behold, truly so it occurred."

21. R. Avigdor b. R. Isaac Kara, "S'licha L'minhat Yom Kippur K'Minhag Prague," in *Sefer ha-D'ma'ot*, ed. S. Bernfeld (Berlin, 1884), II, pp. 160–62. R. Avigdor b. Isaac Kara, who died in 1439, was a rabbi, kabbalist, and liturgical poet. He became famous as a result of his disputations with Christians.

22. See H. J. D. Azulai, *Shem ha-G'dolim ha-Shalem*, sec.: "G'dolim" (New York: Grossman, 1958), p. 66. See S. ibn Verga, *Shevet Yehudah*, ed. Wiener, p. 129.

23. Crescas writes as follows: "Many, including my only son, a perfect lamb I brought up to the sacrificial altar, sanctified the Lord's Name. I yield to God's righteousness, and I will be comforted with a knowledge of his worthy lot and his pleasant fate. There were those among them who jumped from the tower, and before they were halfway down, their bodies had been broken limb from limb. Some fled and sanctified God's Name on the road; the rest converted [to Christianity]. Only a few, who are considered among the respected [members of the community], escaped to the prefects' cities. And [therefore] because of our many sins, there is no one in Barcelona that could be described as Jewish."

24. *D'vei Eliyahu* (Jerusalem, 1968), p. 87.

25. This poem is from a dirge by Don Judah b. Don Isaac Abrabanel, cited in *Sefer ha-D'ma'ot*, II, p. 266.

26. N. Hannover, *Yeven M'zulah* (Tel-Aviv, 1966), p. 38. "And a few women and maidens jumped into the moat adjacent to the citadel and

drowned in the water, lest the Gentiles defile them" (p. 39). "Another incident [occurred] in which a beautiful young maiden [forced to] marry a Cossack, requested that this marriage take place in their house of idolatry beyond the bridge. [The Cossack] agreed to her wishes and brought her to be wed [there] in queenly raiment and with great joy. When she reached the bridge, she jumped into the water and drowned; thus, sanctifying God's Name, may the Lord avenge her." See too the Shach's descriptions of the massacres of 1647 and 1648 in *Shevet Yehudah*, ed. Wiener, pp. 134–39.

27. "The massacre began with a Jewish woman who went to the fields early in the morning to tend the animals there. [It was there that a] treacherous [Gentile] thrust a knife into her. A woman storekeeper, upon witnessing this incident, ran to her fellow Jews crying, 'Let us not betray the living God; let us all instead commit suicide to sanctify His Name thereby making us worthy to enter the world-to-come.' Upon witnessing this, the cantor hurried to the ritual bath to bathe himself. He [then] attired himself in his prayer shawl and phylacteries and recited the [traditional] Confession before Death, with many tears and cries. He then took the knife from the treacherous one and slaughtered his [own] wife and children; and soon after, himself." Translated from the Yiddish by S. Bernfeld, in *Sefer ha-D'ma'ot*, III, pp. 291–92.

28. I. Y. Unterman, *Shevet Miyehudah* (Jerusalem, 1955), pt. I, no. 15. This theme is also demonstrated in the Conservative prayerbook. The incident of ninety-three Bais Yaakov students who took their lives rather than allow themselves to be taken by the Nazis for immoral purposes has been integrated into the High Holiday services. It is spoken of in the most exalted terms. See Ben Zion Bokser, *The High Holiday Prayer Book* (New York: Hebrew Publishing Co., 1959), pp. 434–36. See also Shimoni, D., *Hevlo shel Moshi'ah*, 1951, p. 5.

29. S. Luria, *Yam Shel Sh'lomo*, Baba Kamma, chapter 8, no. 59.

30. See also *Piskei Tos.*, Baba Kamma, *ha-hovel*, no. 215.

31. See above, p. 43.

32. Maimonides, *Yad ha-Hazakah, Hilkhot Ma'akhalot Asurot* 11:7. *Tur, Yoreh De'ah*, chap. 124; *Shulhan Arukh, Yoreh De'ah*, chap. 124, no. 7. See Taz there.

33. E. Oschry, *She'elot Ut'shuvot Mima'makim* (New York, 1959), pt. 1, no. 6.

34. L. Davidowicz in *The War Against the Jews* (New York: Holt, Rinehart & Winston, 1975) notes that the daily statistics of death tabulated in Lodz showed a higher suicide rate among the assimilated German and Czech Jews than among the Polish Jews. See also Irving Rosenbaum, *The Holocaust and Halakhah* (New York: Ktav, 1976), pp. 39–40.

35. S. Goren, "She-elah u'Teshuvah b'nidon giborei Masada," *Or HaMizrach* 7, nos. 3–4 (Tammuz–Elul 1960): 22–27.

36. M. Neriah, "Hitabdut lada'at, giborei Masada l'or ha'Halacha," *Or HaMizrach* 7, nos. 1–2 (Tevet 1961): 8–12.

Chapter 7

1. See *Semaḥot* 2, R. Ishmael's statement, and E. Fleckeles, *T'shuvah Me'ahavah* (Prague, 1781), *Yoreh De'ah*, no. 40. In speaking of a woman who took her own life, Fleckeles says, "Suicide is a serious transgression, most weighty of the weighty and greatest of the great [in its severity]." In a similar vein is the statement *ham'abbed azmo lada'at ein lo ḥelek l'olam haba'*, "he who willfully takes his own life has no share in the world to come." However, this "folk-statement" is not found in any Rabbinic sources.

2. The discussion deals with self-inflicted injury.

3. Rashi, R. Meyuhas b. Elijah, R. Baḥya, R. Solomon b. Abraham Parḥon, R. Joseph Bekhor Shor, Ḥizkuni, R. Jacob Z. Mecklenburg, R. Samson Raphael Hirsch, R. Meir Loeb (Malbim), R. David Z. Hoffman.

4. Naḥmanides, R. David Kimḥi.

5. R. Abraham Ibn Ezra, R. Nissim, Abrabanel, Sforno, R. Moses Al-sheik, R. Samuel David Luzzato, R. Naftali Zvi Yehuda Berlin.

6. See above, p. 9.

7. Ibid.

8. Above, p. 10.

9. Above, p. 8.

10. Above, pp. 10–11.

11. Above, pp. 15–16.

12. Ibid.

13. Above, pp. 20–21.

14. Above, p. 24. Luria's interpretations have wider applicability.

15. Above, p. 39.

16. Above, pp. 45–47.

17. The Christian attitude has apparently been less lenient. It has, however, moderated in recent years due to the influence of psychiatric research. See Excursus III, "Attitudes Toward Suicide in Christianity."

18. E. Durkheim, *Suicide* (Glencoe, Ill., 1951), p. 155; L. Dublin and B. Bunzel, *To Be or Not to Be* (New York: Harrison Smith & Robert Haas, 1933), pp. 119–23, 180–82.

19. Maimonides, *Yad, Hilkhot Ma'akhalot Asurot* 11:7.

20. Above, p. 25.

21. Maimonides, *Yad, Hilkhot Ma'akhalot Asurot* 11:7.

22. In contrast, the Cynic and Stoic schools of philosophy viewed it affirmatively. Under conditions of duress, such as poverty and ill health, some classical sources permitted suicide (Plato, *Laws*, IX) or even advocated it (Pliny the Younger, *Epistles*, I, 22). Judaic sources at most found it inculpable.

23. Above, pp. 21–22.

24. Above, p. 31.

25. Above, pp. 29–30.

26. Above, p. 35.

27. See Excursus IV, "Suicide in Psychiatric Literature."

Excursus I

1. Dov Zlotnick, ed. and trans., *The Tractate "Mourning" (Semahot)*, Yale Judaica Series, vol. XVII (New Haven: Yale University Press, 1966), 2:1.

2. *Halakhot G'dolot, Hilkhot Aveilut;* Alfasi, *Mo'ed Katan* 1254; Maimonides, *Yad, Ebel* 1:11. R. David b. Zimra, *Yad, Ebel* 1:11, poses the question: "If there is no mourning, how is it that the relatives stand in line and the mourner's benediction is recited?" His answer is that "no mourning is observed" because "mourning is an honor bestowed on the deceased, but to stand in line or to recite the mourner's benediction is an act of homage to the Almighty, which is an honor bestowed on the living." The *Kesef Mishnah* and the *Lehem Mishnah* (*Yad, Ebel* 1:11) also feel that Maimonides' view is that mourning is not to honor the living.

3. Nahmanides, *Torat ha-Adam*, pp. 84–86.

4. *Responsa of the Rashba*, V (Vilna, 1884), no. 236. The *Lehem Mishnah* on *Yad, Ebel* 1:11, is of the opinion that the Rashba states that the intentional suicide should be buried to spare the family added humiliation.

5. Y. M. Tukzinski, *Gesher ha-Hayyim*, I (Jerusalem, 1960), p. 174.

6. Leviticus 21:1–4.

7. *Yoreh De'ah* 373.8.

8. Deuteronomy 21:23.

9. *Gilyon Maharsha, Yoreh De'ah* 345, s.v. *u'Manihin*.

10. Y. D. Eisenstein, *Ozar Dinim u'Minhagim* (New York, 1938), p. 197.

11. *She'elot Ut'shuvot Mima'amakim* (New York, 1959), I, no. 6.

12. *Kitvei R. Samuel Mohiliver* (Jerusalem), I, p. 120; *She'elot Ut'shuvot Maharsham* (New York, 1962), I, no. 62. See also A. Rothkoff, *Bernard Revel* (Philadelphia: Jewish Publication Society), pp. 313–14.

13. *Responsa of the Hatam Sofer* (Vienna, 1883), *Yoreh De'ah*, no. 326. "And it is sufficient that in regard to the laws of mourning, the decision of the lenient authority is paramount. However, where the situation involves the halakhic disgrace of a family, the lenient authority, who is in fact impeaching the honor of the children of Abraham, Isaac, and Jacob (if one does not mourn), is not followed."

14. *Kapei Aharon*, II (Jerusalem), *Yoreh De'ah, Hilkhot Aveilut*, no. 16.

15. *Responsa of the Hatam Sofer, Yoreh De'ah*, no. 326.

16. *Responsa ha-Elef L'kha Sh'lomo* (Jerusalem, 1967), *Yoreh De'ah*, no. 300.

17. *Kapei Aharon, loc. cit.*

18. *Responsa Yudah Ya'aleh* (Lemberg, 1873), no. 355.

19. *Responsa Minhat Eliezer* (Breslau, 1922), no. 32.

20. See above, pp. 18–19, for the views of Bahag, Alfasi, and Maimonides.

21. See above, pp. 21–22.

22. R. Judah Aszod, R. Moshe Schick.

Excursus II

Sources in this excursus are cited by A. W. Mair, "Suicide (Greek & Roman)," *Encyclopedia of Religion and Ethics* (1928), 12:26–33. I am indebted to Dr. Louis Feldman, Professor of Classics, Yeshiva University, for his many helpful suggestions with regard to this chapter.

1. Homer, *Odyssey,* XI, 271 ff. Homer does not condemn her (Epikaste's) suicide.

2. *Iliad,* VI, 410; see also Hyginus, *Fabulae* 243, for a similar instance of the suicide of Anticleia, Odysseus' mother, in grief for her son when he had not returned from Troy. Cf. also Aegeus' suicide (Catullus 64, 52 ff.) when he (falsely) learned of the death of his son, Theseus.

3. Servius on Virgil, *Aeneid,* III, 279, and Pausanias, IX, 13, 3.

4. See Lycurgus, *Contra Leokratidem,* 84 ff., with regard to Kodros, the last king of Athens, and Pausanias, I, XXXII, and Euripides, *Herakleidai,* with regard to Makaria, the daughter of Herakles, and Deianeira.

It should be noted that suicide in antiquity due to economic changes is rare. Menippus, the pupil of Diogenes the Cynic, who took his own life because of the loss of his fortune, is exceptional.

5. Herodotus, II, 100.

6. Thucydides, III, 81.

7. *Anabasis,* I, 8.

8. Pausanias, VII, XXI.

9. Herodotus, I, 45.

10. Pindar, *Nemean Odes,* X, 76 ff.

11. "Suicide (Greek & Roman)," p. 28.

12. *Phaedo,* 68A.

13. *Hellenica,* II, III, 56, where the execution of Theramenes through the drinking of hemlock is cited. The most famous case of execution by this means is the death of Socrates (Plato, *Phaedo,* 57A).

14. S. v. *Kunegion.* See also Plato, *Laws,* 873C.

15. Philolaos *ap.* Clement, *Stromateis,* III, 3, p. 186.

16. *Laws,* 865 and 873C–D; *Phaedo,* 62B. Plato (*Laws* IX) permitted suicide, however, when the law required it, and also when men had been struck down by intolerable calamity or had sunk to dire levels of poverty.

17. *Nicomachean Ethics,* V, II (1138a).

18. Diogenes Laertius, IV, 64 f.; Stobaeus, *Florilegium,* CXIX, 19; Stobaeus, II, 264–66; see H. Usener, *Epicurea* (Berlin, 1887–1908), III, 60 (trans. A. E. Taylor).

19. See Mair, "Suicide (Greek & Roman)," p. 30.

20. Diogenes Laertius, VII, 130.

21. Ibid., VII, 28 ff. (suicide of Zeno), VII, 176 (suicide of Cleanthes). This advocacy of suicide was to reach its height under the Roman Empire in the works of Seneca. See further, p. 66.

22. Diogenes Laertius, VI, 18.

23. Cicero, *Pro Sestio*, 48; *Pro Scauro*, III, 1 ff.

24. Livy, I, 57f.

25. Livy, VIII, 9 f; X, 28. See also Polybius, I, 25–26, and Horace, *Odes*, bk. III, for the description of the patriotic suicide of Regulus.

26. Servius, in his commentary on *Aeneid*, XII, 595 ff., indicates that Amata, wife of King Latinus, allegedly a contemporary of Aeneas and of the Trojan War, because she committed suicide by hanging herself with a noose, was, according to the ancient Roman pontifical books, cast out unburied. He quotes Cassius Hemina, the earliest Roman annalist, that Tarquin the Proud (the last Roman king, who was expelled in 510 B.C.E.) ordered the bodies of suicides to be affixed to a cross and that then for the first time it was regarded as disgraceful to commit suicide.

27. Pliny, *Epistles*, I, 22.

28. See ibid., III, 7.

29. Seneca, *Epistles*, LVIII.

30. See Tacitus, *Annals*, VI, 29. See Pliny, *Epistles*, III, 16, where he praises the conduct of Arnia, who encouraged her husband, Caecina Paetus, to commit suicide when his part in a conspiracy against Claudius was discovered.

31. For variations and differences in the procedure of dealing with suicides in Roman law, see Justinian, *Digest*, XLVIII, 21, *De bonis eorum qui ante sententiam vel mortem sibi consciverunt vel accusatorem corruperunt* 3.

32. C. Dublin and B. Bunzel, *To Be or Not to Be* (New York: Harrison Smith & Robert Haas, 1933), p. 183.

Excursus III

Sources through note 14 (with the exception of the personal letter in note 3) are cited by H. J. Rose, "Suicide," *Encyclopedia of Religion and Ethics* (1928), 12:21–23.

1. The two suicides mentioned in the New Testament are those of Judas, Matthew 27:5, and the attempted suicide of Paul's jailor, Acts 16:27.

2. See Justin Martyr, Tertullian, and Cyprian.

3. Christian scholars are careful to differentiate between suicide and martyrdom. "Suicide, properly defined, is always an objective evil; martyrdom, properly defined, is a moral good" (Personal letter from Rev. W. B.

Smith, S.T.D., Professor of Moral Theology, St. Joseph's Seminary, Yonkers, New York, August 9, 1977).

4. Eusebius, *Ecclesiastical History*, VIII, 12.

5. Ibid., VIII, 14.

6. *Epistles*, XXXVIII.

7. In "Suicide," p. 23.

8. *De Civitate Dei*, I, 17.

9. Ibid., chap. 20.

10. Ibid., chap. 21.

11. Ibid., chap. 17.

12. Ibid., chap. 25.

13. Ibid., chap. 26.

14. Norman St. John-Stevas, *The Right to Life* (New York: Holt, Rinehart & Winston, 1963), p. 60.

15. This is very similar to the Aristotelian view on the subject.

16. Cited by Rose, "Suicide," p. 22.

17. I am grateful to my colleague, Fr. Thomas O'Connor, Roman Catholic chaplain at Marlboro Psychiatric Hospital, Marlboro, New Jersey, for his assistance in the translation of these passages.

18. Franco Ferracuti, "Suicide in a Catholic Country," in *Clues to Suicide*, ed. E. Shneidman and N. Farberow (New York: McGraw-Hill, 1957), p. 73.

19. *Pastoral Constitution on the Church in the Modern World (Gaudium et Spes)* (7 Dec. 1965), n. 27. I am indebted to Terrence Cardinal Cooke for his referral of my request as to the Roman Catholic position on suicide to Rev. William B. Smith, S.T.D., professor of moral theology at St. Joseph's Seminary, Dunwoodie, Yonkers, N.Y. Father Smith states as follows: "To be quite frank, much of the theological reasoning is not all that much different from St. Thomas Aquinas (cf. his *Summa Theologiae*, II–II, q. 64–,a.5). If one views human life as a gift from God or an endowment, then Catholic theology sees our domain over life as a useful dominion and not an absolute one. A useful dominion over life is a responsible one; a type of stewardship or governance for which we are accountable—a gift we have on and in trust. Thus, we have no moral right to dispose of any innocent human life directly including our own. One who sees man having absolute moral autonomy over human life, especially his own, will not, and I suppose cannot, accept the view that I just mentioned and the responsibilities and consequences that flow from it." (Personal letter, April 24, 1974).

20. St. John-Stevas, *The Right to Life*, p. 61.

Excursus IV

1. Silvano Arieti, ed., *American Handbook of Psychiatry*, vol. 3 (New York: Basic Books, 1966), p. 116.

2. In *Symposium on Suicide,* ed. Leon Yochelson (Washington, D.C.: George Washington University School of Medicine, 1965).

3. George Murphy, "Suicide and the Right to Die," *American Journal of Psychiatry* 130 (April 1973): 472.

4. Karl Abraham, "Notes on the Psycho-Analytical Investigation and Treatment of Manic Depressive Insanity and Allied Conditions," in *On Character and Libido Development* (New York: Norton, 1966), p. 17.

5. *Selected Papers on Psycho-Analysis* (London: Hogarth Press, 1927), p. 144.

6. Sigmund Freud, *Standard Edition of the Complete Psychological Works,* trans. and ed. by James Strachey (London: Hogarth Press, 1953–65), 6:181.

7. Introjection is the withdrawal of psychic energy from an object and directing it upon the mental image of the object. Definitions in this chapter are taken from Leland E. Hinsie and Robert Jean Campbell, eds., *Psychiatric Dictionary,* 3rd ed. (New York: Oxford University Press, 1960).

8. Freud, *Standard Edition,* 14:247–52.

9. Ibid., 19:53.

10. Ibid., 18:162.

11. Ibid., pp. 46–49.

12. Karl Menninger, *Man Against Himself* (New York: Harcourt, Brace, 1938), p. 82.

13. O. Fenichel, *The Psychoanalytic Theory of Neurosis* (New York: Norton, 1945), p. 400.

14. Bruno Klopfer, "Suicide: The Jungian Point of View," in *The Cry for Help,* ed. N. Farberow and E. Shneidman (New York: McGraw-Hill, 1961), pp. 193–203.

15. A Jungian archetype which is preexistent and superordinate to every form of manifestation of the motherly.

16. Farberow and Shneidman, *The Cry for Help,* p. 293.

17. H. L. Ansbacher, "Suicide: The Adlerian Point of View," in ibid., pp. 204–19.

18. Alfred Adler, *Problems of Neurosis* (London: Routledge & Kegan Paul, 1920), p. 55.

19. H. S. Sullivan, *Clinical Studies in Psychiatry* (New York: Norton, 1956).

20. Farberow and Schneidman, *The Cry for Help,* p. 295.

21. L. De Rosis, "Suicide: The Horney Point of View," in ibid., pp. 236–54. See also Karen Horney, *Neurosis and Human Growth* (New York: Norton, 1950).

22. A description of suicide prevention agencies and their location is found in *The Cry for Help,* pp. 136–49.

23. The outstanding sociological study of suicide is that of Emile Durkheim. Durkheim posits three categories of suicide: 1) Egoistic suicide, which results from an individual's inability to integrate himself into society, 2) altruistic suicide, wherein the individual is highly integrated into his society.

Suicide results in this situation from intense religious or political commitments, and 3) anomic suicide which results from a paucity of restriction of the individual by society. In his work, Durkheim tabulates these different types and their various manifestations; see *Suicide*, ed. J. Simpson, trans. J. A. Spaulding and J. Simpson (The Free Press, Glencoe, IL, 1951).

Appendix

1. *Semahot* 2:1–5.
2. J. Ayash, *Shevet Yehudah* (Leghorn, 1783), *Yoreh De'ah*, no. 345.
3. M. Sofer, *Responsa Hatam Sofer* (Vienna, 1883), *Yoreh De'ah*, no. 326.
4. H. Pontremoli, *Zapikhit Bidvash* (Salonika, 1848), no. 67, as cited in *Sede Hemed*, s.v. *avelut*, no. 123.
5. *P'at ha-Sadeh*, Appendix to *Sedeh Hemed* (New York, 1962), s.v. *avelut*, no. 17.
6. Tos. *Gittin* 57b, s.v. *kafzu*.
7. S. Luria, *Yam Shel Sh'lomo* (Prague, 1715), *Baba Kamma*, chap. 8, no. 59.
8. Tos. *Abodah Zarah* 18a, s.v. *v'al*.
9. *Kiddushin* 81b.
10. William G. Braude, *The Midrash on Psalms* (New Haven: Yale University Press, 1959), pt. 1, 11; 7.
11. S. Kluger, *Responsa ha-Elef L'cha Sh'lomo* (Jerusalem, 1967), *Yoreh De'ah*, no. 301.
12. *Responsa Maharam Schick*, (Munkács, 1881), *Yoreh De'ah*, no. 346.
13. A. Kobo, *Responsa Sha'ar Asher* (Salonika, 1877).
14. H. J. Azulai, *Responsa Hayyim Sha'al* (Leghorn, 1772), Responsa 46.
15. M. Banet, *Responsa Parshat Mordecai* (Sighet, 1889), *Yoreh De'ah*, no. 25.
16. S. Berlin, *Responsa Besamim Rosh* (Berlin, 1793), no. 345.
17. S. Kluger, *Responsa Tuv Ta'am va'Da'at*, 3rd ser. (New York, n.d.), *Hilkhot Aveilut*, no. 202.
18. M. Sofer, *Responsa of the Hatam Sofer* (Pressburg, 1858), *Eben HaEzer*, no. 69.
19. *Hullin* 94a.
20. Ibid.
21. *Berakhot* 23a.
22. H. H. Medini, *Sdei Hemed*, section on *Aveilut*, no. 121.
23. A. Azriel, *Responsa Kapei Aharon* II, (Jerusalem, 1898), *Hilkhot Aveilut*, no. 16.
24. Y. Lapronti, *Pahad Yizhak* (Venice, 1831), letter *mem*, no. 1.
25. J. M. Epstein, *Arukh ha-Shulhan* (New York, 1901), *Yoreh De'ah*, no. 345, par. 5.

26. *Ketubot* 103b.
27. *Abodah Zarah* 18a.
28. *Ta'anit* 29a.

Bibliographical Essay

1. Budapest, 1879.
2. *Monatsschrift fuer Geschichte und Wissenschaft des Judentums* 55 (1911): 287–95.
3. "Suicide," *Encyclopaedia Judaica* (1972) 15:489–90.
4. *Gittin* 57b *Lamentations Rabbah* 1:45.
5. "Suicide in Jewish Law," *Encyclopaedia Judaica* (1974), 15:490–91.
6. *B'ohalei Shem* (Jerusalem, 1963), pp. 82–96.
7. *Judaism* 10, no. 2 (1961): 160–70.
8. *Modern Medicine and Jewish Law,* Studies in Torah Judaism (New York: Yeshiva University Press, 1972), pp. 177–93.
9. *Law and Theology in Judaism* (New York: Ktav, 1974), pp. 80–93.
10. (New York: Jonathan David, 1969), pp. 215–20.
11. (New York: 1974), pp. 4, 14, 28, 74, 120, 131.
12. *Ah L'zarah* (1939), and *Kol Bo Al Aveilut* (New York, 1956).
13. J. M. Tuktzinski, *Gesher ha-Hayyim* (Jerusalem, 1960), pp. 269–73.
14. *Mishpatim L'yisrael* (Jerusalem: Machon Harry Fischel L'drishat ha-Talmud, 1956), pp. 243–57, 307–308.
15. S. Ibn Verga, *Shevet Yehudah,* ed. M. Wiener (1855) and A. Schochat (Jerusalem, 1947); Yoseph HaKohen HaRofe, *Emek ha-Bakha,* (Jerusalem, 1956); N. Hannover, *Yeven M'zulah* (Tel-Aviv, 1966); E. Capsali, *Likkutim Shonim MiSefer de-vei Eliyahu* (Padua, 1869).
16. S. Bernfeld, *Sefer ha-D'ma'ot* (Berlin, 1926); A. M. Habermann, *Sefer Gezerot Ashkenaz v'Zarfat* (Jerusalem, 1946); Y. Heilprin, *Sefer ha-Gevurah* (Tel-Aviv, 1950).

Select Bibliography

Abraham, Karl. *Selected Papers on Psycho-Analysis.* London: Hogarth Press, 1927.

Adler, A. *Problems of Neurosis.* London: Routledge & Kegan Paul, 1920.

Ansbacher, Hile, and Rowena R. Ansbacher, eds. *The Individual Psychology of Alfred Adler.* New York: Basic Books, 1956.

Arieti, Silvano, ed. *American Handbook of Psychiatry.* Vol. 3. New York: Basic Books, 1966.

Ashtor, E. *Jews in Moslem Spain.* Vol. 1. Trans. by A. Klein. Philadelphia: Jewish Publication Society, 1973.

Augustine, Saint. *City of God.* Trans. by M. Dods. New York: Random House, 1950.

Bokser, B. Z., trans. *High Holiday Prayer Book.* New York: Hebrew Publishing Co., 1959.

Braude, William, ed. *Pesikta Rabbati.* New Haven: Yale University Press, 1968.

Chavel, C., ed. and trans. *Commentary of Nahmanides on Genesis.* New York: Shilo Publishing House, 1971.

Davidowicz, Lucy S. *The War Against the Jews.* New York: Holt, Rinehart & Winston, 1975.

Dublin, L., and B. Bunzel. *To Be or Not to Be.* New York: Harrison Smith & Robert Haas, 1933.

Durkheim, E. *Suicide.* Glencoe, Ill: Free Press, 1951.

Farberow, N., and E. Shneidman. *Clues to Suicide.* Toronto: McGraw-Hill, Blaikston Division, 1957.

————, eds. *The Cry for Help.* New York: McGraw-Hill, 1961.

Felder, Aaron. *Yesodei Smochos.* New York, 1974.

Finkelstein, L. *The Pharisees.* Philadelphia: Jewish Publication Society, 1940.

Freud, S. *Standard Edition of the Complete Psychological Works.*

Trans. and edited by James Strachey. London: Hogarth Press, 1953–65.

Goitein, S. D. *Jews and Arabs*. 3rd ed. New York: Schocken Books, 1974.

Haring, B. *The Law of Christ*. Vol. 3. Westminster, Md.: Newman, 1966.

Hinsie, Leslie, and R. J. Campbell. *Psychiatric Dictionary*. 3rd ed. New York: Oxford University Press, 1960.

Horney, Karen. *Neurosis and Human Growth*. New York: Norton, 1950.

Ibn Daud, Abraham. *Sefer Ha-Qabbalah*. Edited by G. D. Cohen. Philadelphia: Jewish Publication Society, 1967.

Jakobovits, Immanuel. *Jewish Medical Ethics*. New York: Bloch Publishing Co., 1959.

Lamm, Maurice. *The Jewish Way in Death and Mourning*. New York: Jonathan David, 1969.

Menninger, K. *Man Against Himself*. New York: Harcourt Brace, 1938.

Milt, H. *The Roots of Suicide*. Merck, Sharp, Dohme.

National Conference of Catholic Bishops. *Basic Teachings for Catholic Religious Education*. Washington, D.C.: Publications Office of the United States Catholic Conference, 1973.

Novak, David. *Law and Theology in Judaism*. New York: Ktav Publishing House, 1974.

Rosenbaum, Irving. *The Holocaust and Halakha*. New York: Ktav Publishing House, 1976.

Rosner, Fred. *Modern Medicine and Jewish Law*. Studies in Torah Judaism, vol. 13. New York: Yeshiva University Press, 1972.

Roth, A. *Eine Studie ueber den Selbstmord vom juedischen Standpunkte*. Budapest, 1879.

Rothkoff, A. *Bernard Revel*. Philadelphia: Jewish Publication Society, 1972.

St. John-Stevas, N. *The Right to Life*. New York: Holt, Rinehart & Winston, 1964.

Sullivan, Henry S. *Clinical Studies in Psychiatry*. New York: Norton, 1956.

St. Thomas Aquinas, Saint. *Summa Theologica.*

Yochelson, Leon, ed. *Symposium on Suicide.* Washington, D. C.: George Washington University School of Medicine, 1967.

Zlotnick, D., ed. and trans. *The Tractate "Mourning."* Yale Judaica Series, vol. 17. New Haven: Yale University Press, 1966.

Articles

Abraham, Karl. "Notes on the Psycho-Analytical Investigation and Treatment of Manic Depressive Insanity and Allied Conditions." In *On Character and Libido Development.* New York: Norton, 1966.

Cohn, Haim H. "Suicide in Jewish Law." In *Encyclopaedia Judaica* (1972), Vol. 15.

Daube, David. "Josephus on Suicide and Liability of Depositee." In *Libro Jubilar de Victor Andres Belaunde, Mercurio Peruano,* pp. 231–41. Lima, 1963.

Hankoff, L. D. "The Theme of Suicide in the Works of Flavius Josephus." *Clio Medica* 2, no. 1 (1976): 15–24.

Lieberman, Saul. "Some Aspects of After Life in Early Rabbinic Literature." In *Harry A. Wolfson Jubilee Volume,* vol. 2. Jerusalem: American Academy for Jewish Research, 1956.

Mair, A. W. "Suicide (Greek and Roman)." In *Encyclopedia of Religion and Ethics* (1928), vol. 12.

Nelson, B. "Suicide Prevention: N.I.M.H. Wants More Attention for Taboo Subject." *Science* 161 (August 1968): 766–67.

Perls, A. "Der Selbstmord nach der Halacha." *Monatsschrift fuer Geschichte und Wissenschaft des Judentums* 55 (1911): 287–95.

Rabinowitz, L. I. "Suicide." In *Encyclopaedia Judaica* (1972), vol. 15.

Reines, C. W. "The Jewish View of Suicide." *Judaism* 10, no. 2 (1961): 160–70.

Rose, H. J. "Suicide." In *Encyclopedia of Religion and Ethics* (1928), vol. 12.

Solomon, P. "The Burden of Responsibility in Suicide and Homicide." *Journal of the American Medical Association* 199 (January 1967): 321–24.

Basic Texts

The Apocrypha of the Old Testament. Revised Standard Version. New York: Thomas Nelson & Sons, 1957.

Babylonian Talmud. London: Soncino Press, 1936.

The Holy Scriptures. Philadelphia: Jewish Publication Society, 1955.

Midrash Rabbah. London: Soncino Press, 1939.

The New Testament. Trans. by Edgar J. Goodspeed. Chicago: University of Chicago Press, 1923.

The Tanach and Its Expounders

Abrabanel, Don Isaac. *Commentary on the Torah.* Jerusalem, 1964.

———. *Commentary on the Prophets and Writings.* Jerusalem, 1955.

Alshekh, Moses. *Mar'ot ha-Zov'ot, Samuel.* Jerusalem, 1964.

———. *Torat Moshe.* Amsterdam, 1777.

Baḥya ben Asher. *Commentary on the Torah, Genesis.* ed. C. B. Chavel. Jerusalem: Mossad Harav Kook, 1966.

Bekhor Shor, J. *Commentary on the Torah.* Ed. A. Jellinek. Jerusalem, 1956.

Berlin, N. Z. J. *Ha-Emek Davar.* Jerusalem, 1970.

Gerondi, J. *Commentary on the Torah.* Ed. A Feldman. Jerusalem, 1965.

Hezekiah ben Mano'ah. *Commentary of Hizkuni.* In *Mikra'ot G'dolot.* New York: Schulsinger, 1950.

Hirsch, S. R. *Commentary on the Torah.* Trans. into English by J. Halevi. London, 1956–62.

Hoffman, D. Z. *Commentary on Genesis.* Bene-Berak, n.d.

Jacob ben Asher. *Lengthy Commentary of the Tur on the Torah.* Jerusalem, 1964.

Malbim, M. L. *Torat Elokim.*

Mecklenburg, J. Z. *Ha-K'tav v'ha-Kabbalah.* Frankfurt am Main, 1850.

Meyuchas b. Elijah. *Commentary of R. Meyuchas on Genesis.* Jerusalem, 1968.

Mikra'ot G'dolot. New York: Pardes, 1951.

————. New York: Schulsinger, 1950.

Parḥon, S. *Mahberet ha-Arukh*. Pressburg, 1844.

Rabboteinu Ba'alei ha-Tosafot al ha-Torah. Jerusalem: Lewin-Epstein, 1967.

Saadia (ben Joseph) Gaon. *Commentary of R. Saadia Gaon on the Torah*. ed. Y. Kapah. Jerusalem, 1963.

Tanna'itic and Amoraitic Sources

Babylonian Talmud, with all the Commentaries, Vilna.

Genesis Rabbah. Ed. Theodore Albeck. Berlin, 1926–29.

Jerusalem Talmud, with all the Commentaries. New York: Ot-zar ha Seforim, 1959.

Midrash ha-Gadol on the Torah: Genesis. Ed. M. Margolis. Jerusalem, 1964.

Midrash Samuel. Ed. S. Buber. Jerusalem, 1965.

Mishneh Tiferet Yisrael with all the Commentaries. New York: Pardes, 1953.

Pesikta Rabbati. Ed. M. Friedmann. Tel-Aviv, 1963.

Pirkei de-Rabbi Eliezer, with Commentary of D. Luria. New York, 1946.

Semaḥot. Ed. M. Higger. New York, 1931.

Sources of the Geonim and Rishonim

Adret, Solomon ben Abraham. *Responsa of the Rashba*. Vilna, 1884.

Asher ben Jehiel. *Commentary* in *Babylonian Talmud*. Vilna edition.

Gerondi, J. *Ḥiddushei R. Jonah on Sanhedrin*. Jerusalem, 1968.

Halakhot G'dolot. Rome MS. Berlin, 1888.

Halakhot G'dolot. Jerusalem, 1972.

Isaac of Corbeil. *Amudei ha-Golah*. Israel, 1959.

Jacob b. Asher. *Turim Tur, Yoreh De'ah*. Jerusalem: Makhon Hatam Sofer, 1966.

Karo, Joseph. *Shulḥan Arukh*. New York, 1967. Photo-offset of the Vilna 1891 edition.

Maimonides, M. *Mishnah Torah*. New York: Schulsinger, 1947.

Meir ben Barukh of Rothenburg. *T'shuvot P'sakim UMinhagim.* Ed. I. Z. Cahana. Jerusalem, 1960.

Naḥmanides. *Torat Ha-Adam, Kitvei Ramban.* Ed. C. B. Chavel. Jerusalem: Mosad Harav Kook, 1964.

Ozar ha-Geonim: Sanhedrin. Ed. H. Tauber. Jerusalem, 1967.

Sa'adia (ben Joseph). *Emunot V'De'ot.* Ed. Y. Karaḥ. Jerusalem, 1970.

Works of the Later Generations

Aszod, Judah. *Yudah Ya'aleh, Yoreh De'ah.* Lemberg and Pressburg, 1873.

Ayash, J. *Shevet Yehudah, Yoreh De'ah.* Leghorn, 1783.

Azriel, A. *Kapei Aharon.* Vol. 2. Jerusalem, 1898.

Azulai, H. *Birkei Yoseph, Yoreh De'ah.* Leghorn, 1774

———. *Ḥayyim Sha'al.* Leghorn, 1792.

———. *Shem ha-Gadolim ha-Shalem.* New York: Grossman, 1958.

Banet, M. *Parshat Mordechai, Yoreh De'ah.* Sighet, 1889.

Berlin, S. *Besamin Rosh, Yoreh De'ah.* Berlin, 1793.

Epstein, J. M. *Arukh ha-Shulḥan.* New York, 1961.

Fleckeles, E. *T'shuvah Me'ahavah, Yoreh De'ah.* Prague, 1781.

Ganzfried, S. *Kizzur Shulḥan Arukh.* Jerusalem: Mosad Harav Kook, 1955.

Ginzburg, J. M. *Mispatim L'Yisrael.* Jerusalem: Makhon Harry Fischel, 1956.

Greenwald, Y. *Akh L'zarah.* St. Louis, 1939.

———. *Kol-Bo al Aveilut.* New York, 1956.

Hildesheimer, A. *Responsa, Yoreh De'ah.* Tel-Aviv, 1969.

Kluger, S. *Tuv Ta'am Va'daat.* Third Series. New York: Grossman, n.d.

———. *Ha-Elef L'cha Shlomo.* Jerusalem, 1967.

Kobo, A. *Sha'ar Asher, Yoreh De'ah.* Salonica, 1877.

Kook, A. I. *Mishpat Cohen.* Jerusalem, 1937.

Lampronti, I. *Paḥad Yizhak.* Venice, 1831.

Luria, S. *Yam Shel Shlomo, Baba Kamma.* Prague, 1715.

Margolioth, E. S. *Bet Ephraim, Yoreh De'ah.* Israel, 1968.

Medini, H. H. *Sedeh Ḥemed.* Warsaw, 1891.

Oschry, E. *She'elot Ut'shuvot Hima'amakim.* New York, 1959.

Pontremoli, H. *Zapikhit Bidvash.* Salonika, 1848.

Posek, H. *Hillel Omer, Yoreh De'ah.* Tel-Aviv: Bar-Yehudah, 1956.
Reischer, J. *Sh'vut Ya'akov, Yoreh De'ah.* Prague, 1689.
Schapiro, H. E. *Minḥat Eliezer.* Breslau, 1922.
Schick, M. *Responsa of Maharam Schick, Yoreh De'ah.* Munkács, 1882.
————. *Responsa of Marsham.* Vol. 6. Jerusalem, 1968.
Sofer, M. *Responsa of the Ḥatam Sofer, Yoreh De'ah.*Vienna, 1895.
————. *Responsa of the Ḥatam Sofer, Eben HaEzer* Pressburg, 1858.
Tuktzinski, J. M. *Gesher ha-Ḥayyim.* Jerusalem, 1960.

Articles
Gershuni, Judah. "Hayalei Yisrael hamistaknim neged p'kudah shel ha-kazin im yesh miẓvah l'hazilam." *Or Hamizrach* 21 (1972): 3–8.
————. "Miragel l'tovat hazibur shenitpas im rasha'i l'abed azmo la'da'at." *Or Hamizrach* 21 (1972): 218–22.
Goren, Sh'lomo. "She'elah u'Tshuva b'nidon giborei Masada." *Or Hamizrach* 7, nos. 3–4 (Tammuz–Elul 1960): 22–27.
————. "G'vurat Masada L'or ha-Halakha." *Maḥana'im* 87 (Kislev 1964): 7–12.
Nedava, Yosef. "Ba'ayat ha-hitabdut ba'amim u'v'Yisrael." *Mishpat V'kalkala* 3 (1957): 87–100.
Neriah, Moshe Zevi. "Hitabdut la'daat, giborei Masada l'or ha-halakhah." *Or Hamizrach* 8, nos. 1–2 (Tevet 1961): 8–12.
Rabinowitz, Louis Isaac. "Hitabdut shel ha-kana'im b'Masada." *Sinai* 55 (1964): 329–32.
Rabinowitz, Zevi. "Ibud azmo la'da'at b'einei ha-Yahadut." *Harofe Ha-ivri* 34, nos. 1–2 (1961): 153–56.
Reines, H. Z. "Hitabdut Mida'at bamikra uv'safrut ha-Rabbanit." In *Oholei Shem,* pp. 82–96. Jerusalem and New York, 1963.

Historical Works
Ben Zev, J. *Ha-Yehudim Ba'arav.* Jerusalem, 1957.
Bernfeld, S. *Sefer ha-D'ma'ot.* Berlin, 1886.
Capsali, E. *Likkutim Shonim Misefer de'vei Eliyahu.* Padua, 1869.

Habermann, A. M. *Gezerot Ashkenaz v'Zarfat.* Jerusalem, 1946.

Hannov, N. *Yeven M'zulah.* Tel-Aviv, 1966.

Heilperin, Y. *Sefer ha-Gevurah.* Tel-Aviv, 1950.

Hirshberg, C. Z. *Yisrael Ba'arav.* Tel-Aviv, 1946.

Ibn Verga, Solomon. *Shevet Yehudah.* Ed. Wiener. Jerusalem, 1949.

Joseph Ha-Kohen ha-Rofe. *Emek ha-Bakha.* Jerusalem, 1956.

Additional Sources

Epstein, Baruch ha-Levi. *Torah Temimah.* Vol. 1 Tel-Aviv, 1956.

Hyman, A. M. *Ha-Torah ha-Ketubah v'ha-Mesurah.* Tel-Aviv, 1937–40.

Kasher, M. M. *Torah Shelemah.* Vol. 2. Jerusalem, 1924.

Kasher, S. *Peshuto shel Mikra.* 2 vols. Jerusalem, 1963–68.

Afterword

Some brief thoughts are appropriate with reference to the research. One is impressed by the tremendous value placed on life in the Jewish tradition. Unless one specifically negates its value through witnesses and a clear statement to the effect that he will take his own life, the assumption clearly is that life is so precious that forces beyond the individual's control (often inner psychic ones) impel him to act in a suicidal manner.

The view represented herein, that under no circumstances should the individual actively inflict harm on himself at any time, is a clear affirmation of the principle of the ownership of life by the Supreme Being who has granted that life. Those who feel that actively inflicting harm on oneself is meritorious behavior when done under conditions of martyrdom assume that life, when it is called upon to violate the essential foundations which evidence the presence of the Supreme Being in our lives, becomes untenable. The very purpose of that life granted to us by the Almighty has been vitiated.

This of course carries with it tremendous implications in our daily relationships with those who have been granted life. This affirmation of life is at the root of all human relationships and remains as the essential element of most systems of human organization. It becomes the critical backdrop in measuring the effects and goals of family life, government, medicine, education and all other vital areas of interaction.

The understanding from Jewish sources vis-à-vis suicide, whose influence is clearly shown in that of other faiths, demonstrates that faith in the Grantor of life is the essential foundation on which all human existence is founded.

For unless one accepts the truth of the verse in Genesis "and God created man in His own image" suicide does not pose a substantial ethical dilemma. It is when it is seen as a denial and contradiction of that verse that the theological and ethical problems become manifest. Judaism in its axiomatic acceptance of human life as a manifestation of divine beneficence sees suicide as a renunciation of that principle. The Halakha therefore indicates that when suicide is a culpable act it constitutes renunciation, when it isn't, it is either an aberration or an act of great moral courage. The Halakha of suicide is the manifestation of the Jewish reverence for life and the sacred responsibility which man has to treasure and enhance it.

Index to Biblical
and Talmudic References

General Index